Innuendo Non Troppo
The Work of Gregory Barsamian

David J. Brown   The Contemporary Arts Center, Cincinnati

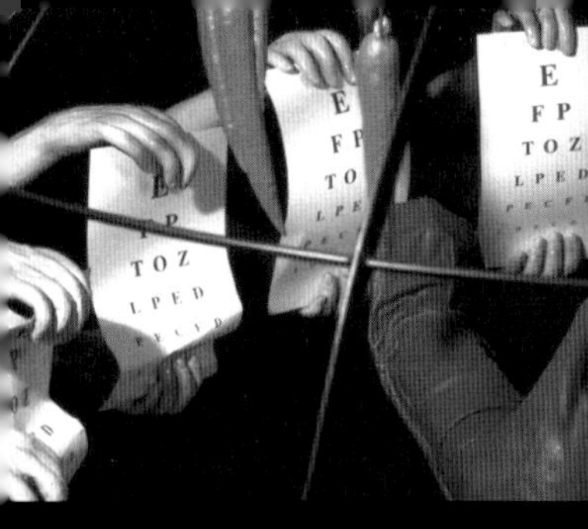

This catalogue contains several animations of the artist's work. Located along the left margin, these sequences can be activated by flipping the pages with your thumb and forefinger.

in•nū•en′dō, *noun*
An indirect or subtle implication in expression.

nōn trōp′pō, *adverb & adjective*
In music, moderately; fast but not too fast.

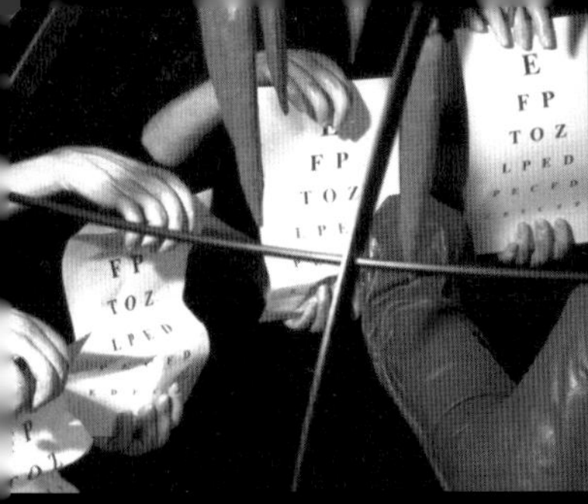

Barsamian's Studio, Brooklyn, NY

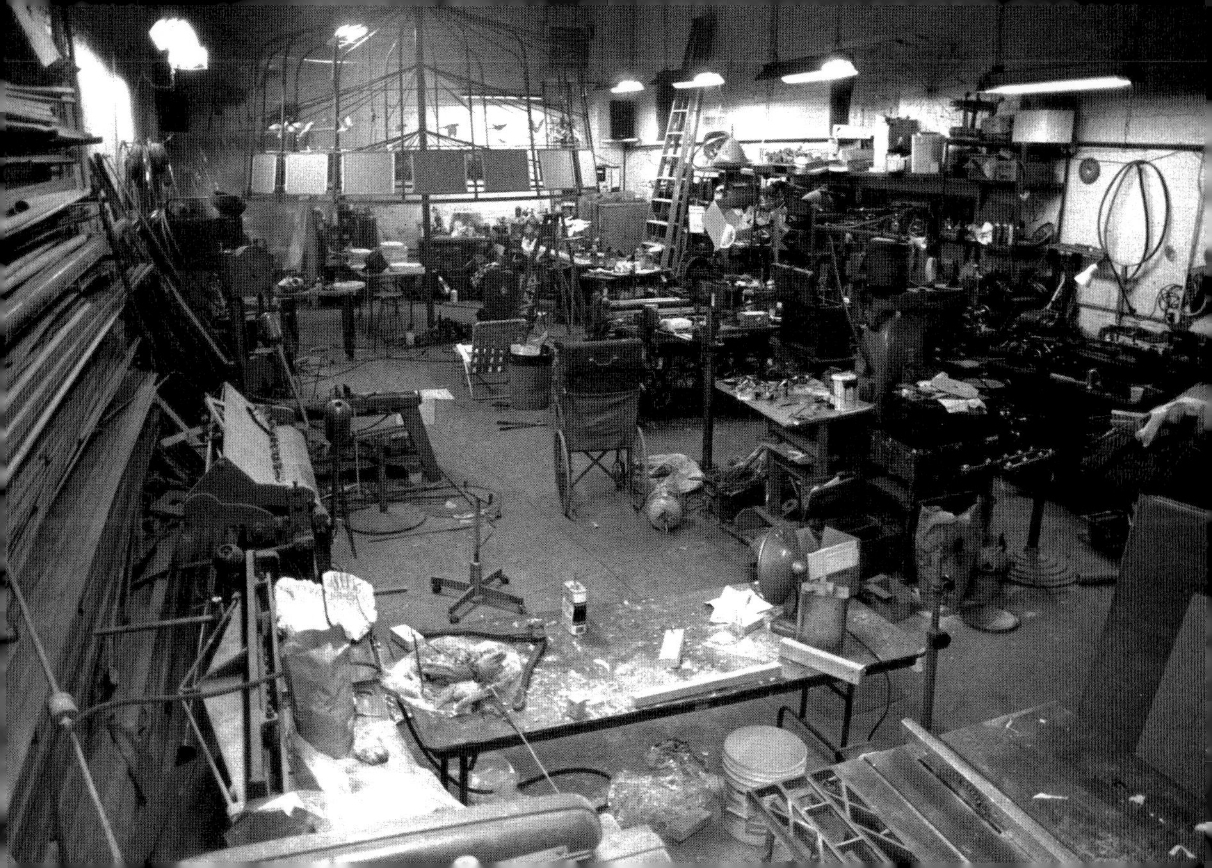

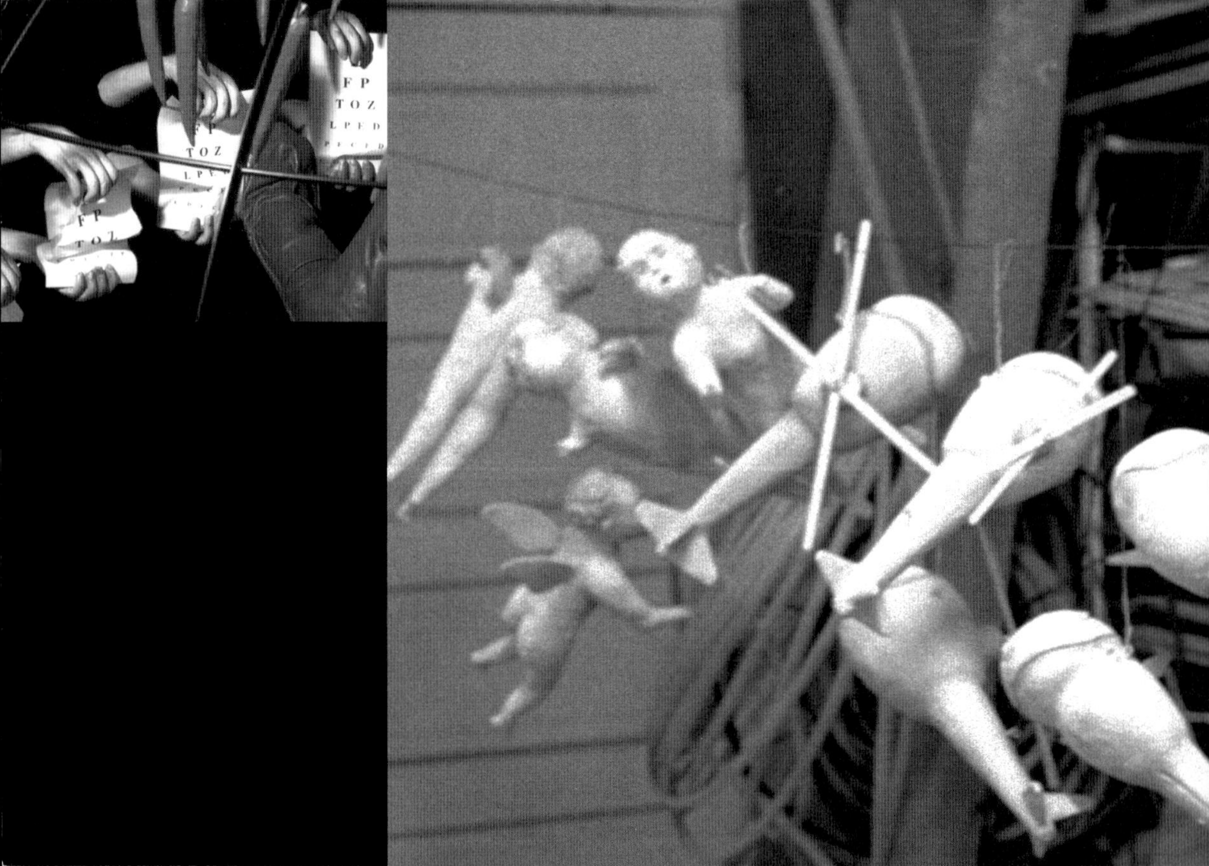
F P
T O Z
L P E D
P E C F D

Tour of the Exhibition

The Contemporary Arts Center
Cincinnati, Ohio
5 September - 1 November 1998

The Arkansas Art Center
Little Rock, Arkansas
22 January - 29 March 1999

Polk Museum of Art
Lakeland, Florida
17 April - 27 June 1999

Anderson Gallery
Virginia Commonwealth University
Richmond, Virginia
15 August - 1 November 1999

Boise Art Museum
Boise, Idaho
4 December - 13 February 2000

San Jose Museum of Art
San Jose, California
16 April - 25 June 2000

Putti *(work in progress)*

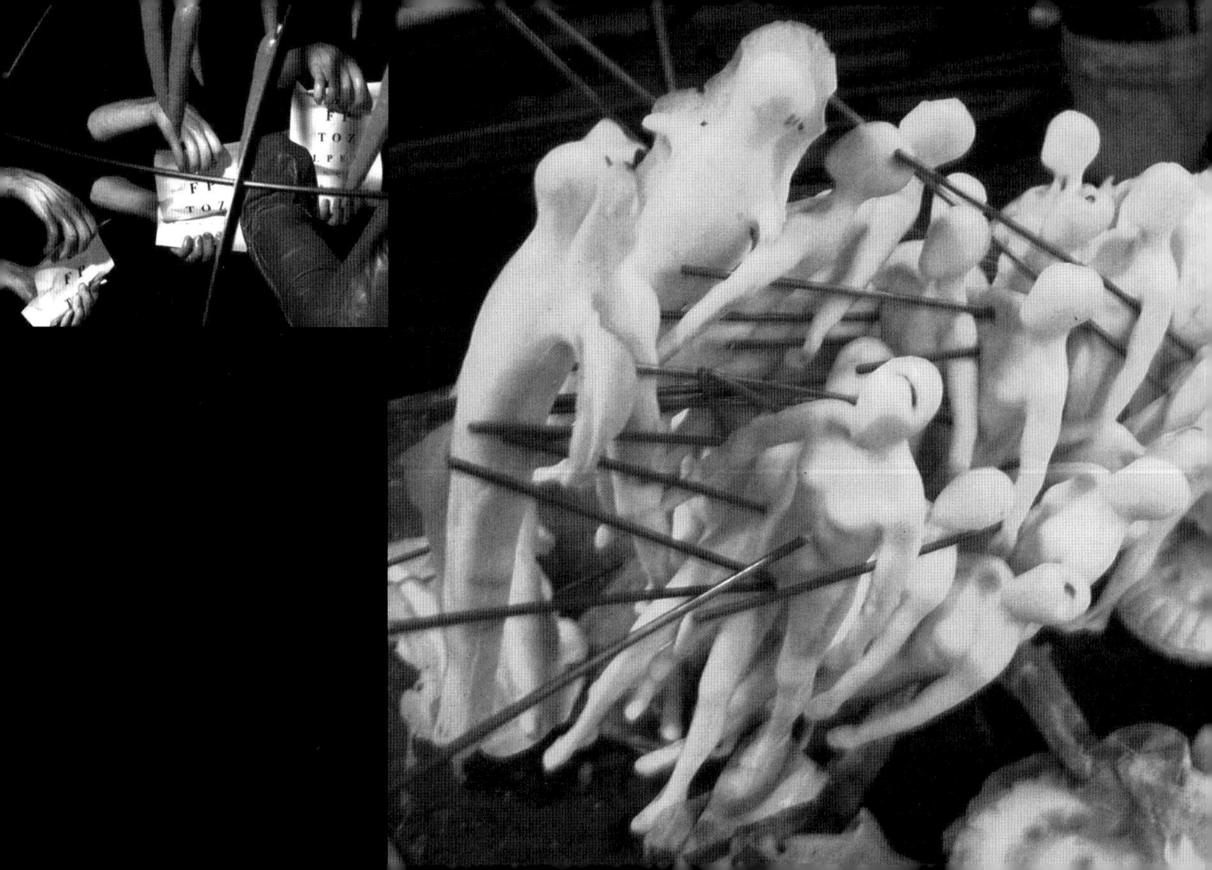

Acknowledgements

In 1991, the Contemporary Arts Center presented a popular group exhibition organized by Jan Riley entitled **Mechanika**. At the center of the exhibition was a sculpture by Gregory Barsamian that at first must have seemed out of place. For in a gallery filled with works meant to evoke an automated, cybernetic world, here was alchemy and magic–a vision ephemeral yet real, as real as the dream that startles us awake.

Such an intriguing and original a work demanded deeper understanding. Since his first day at the CAC in 1996, Curator David Brown has championed a more complete examination of Barsamian's working methods and range of concerns. This publication and the exhibition it documents are a tribute not only to the artist but also to Brown's dedication to Barsamian's art. Without his unflagging attention, the show, its national tour, and this catalogue would not have been possible.

Die Falle (work in progress)

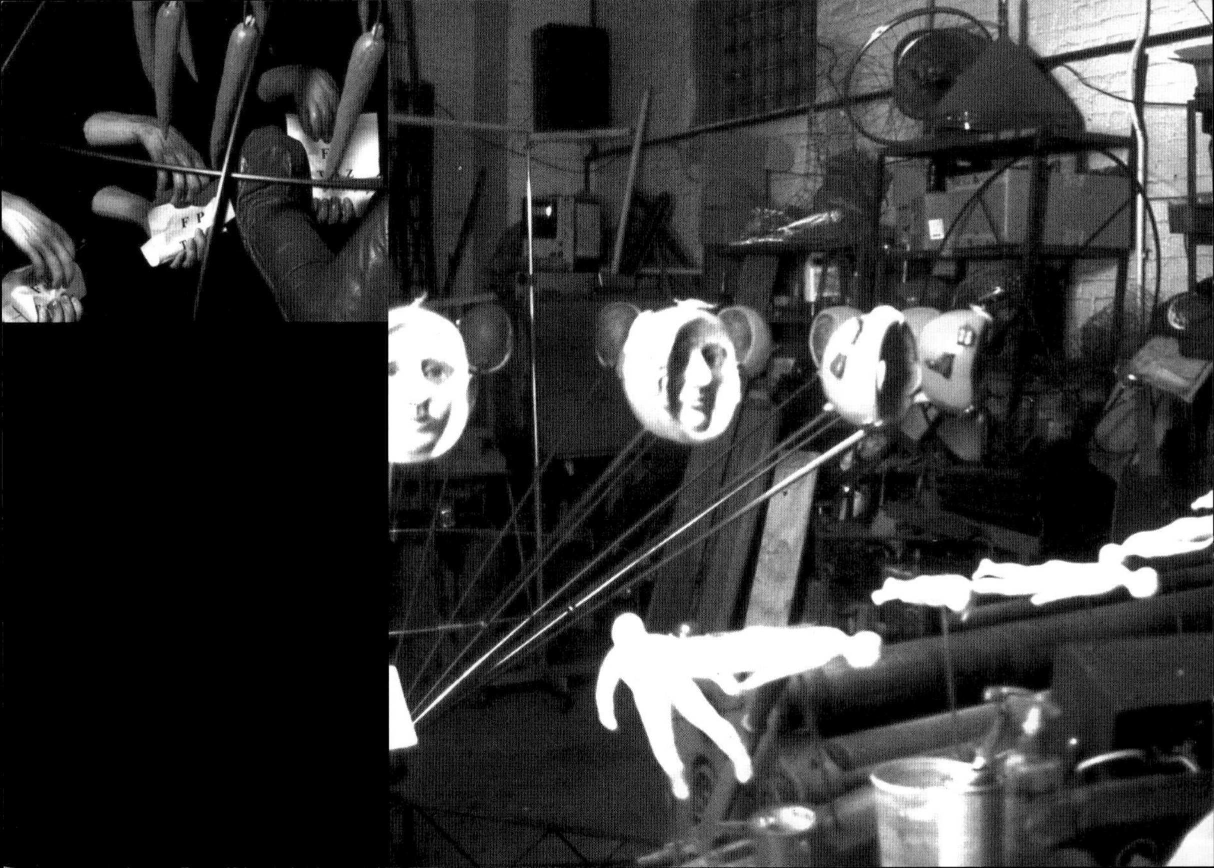

The entire CAC staff provided additional support, particularly Leah Stoddard, who prepared the catalogue information and handled exhibition tour details, and Kim Humphries, who designed the installation.

On behalf of the members and trustees of the CAC, I also thank the many others who have made this project a success. Funding for the exhibition and tour was provided by Star Bank, where Jerry Grundhofer, David Moffett, and Phyllis Slusher have helped to forge a true partnership between business and the arts. A generous grant from the Elizabeth Firestone-Graham Foundation made the exhibition catalogue possible, and we thank Charles D'Arcy for his kind assistance.

While many of the objects included are new works specifically made for the exhibition, crucial loans were made by Raymond and Simon Wang of Taipei, Taiwan, and Irvine, California and Howard Tullman of Chicago. Penelope Schmidt of Schmidt Bingham Gallery, New York, was also of

The Scream and ***Die Falle*** *(work in progress)*

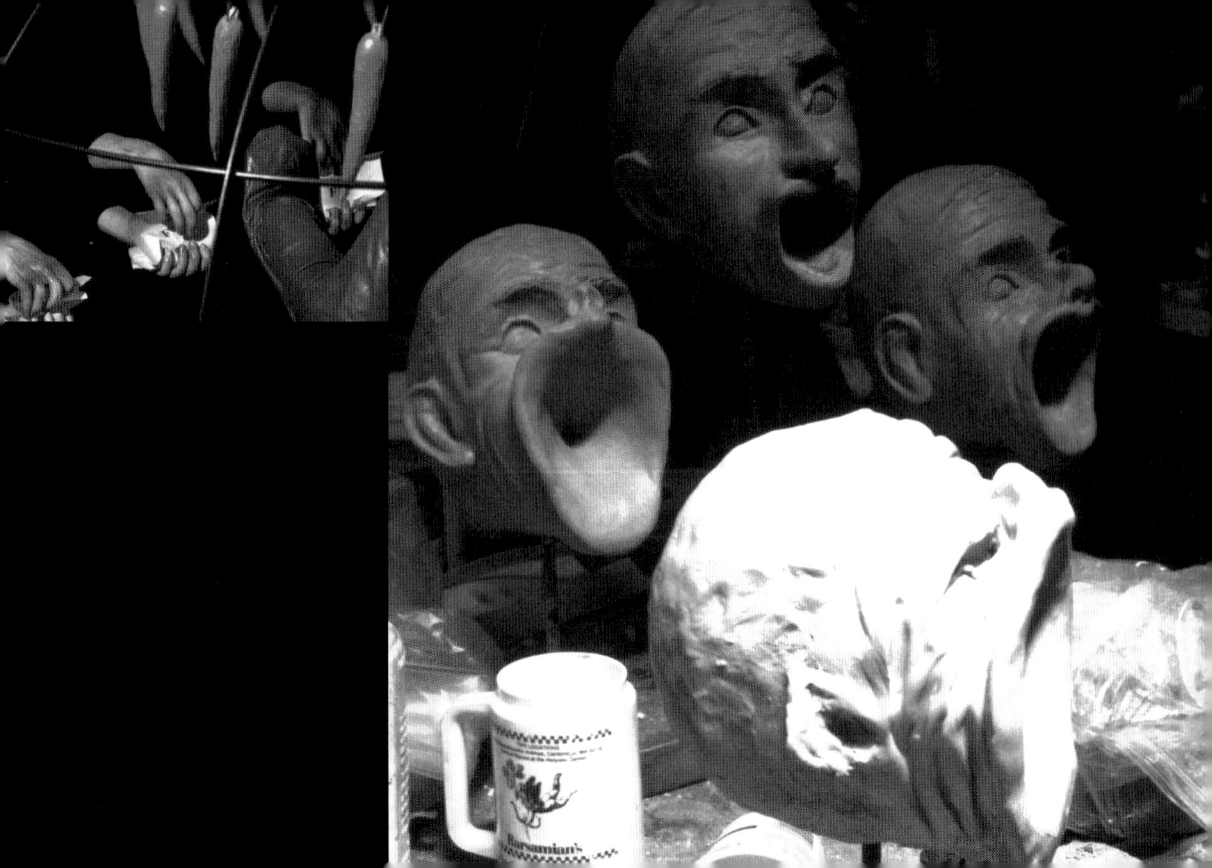

extraordinary assistance; she has long been an enthusiastic supporter of Barsamian and his work. We also thank Robin Perl of Perlgraphic, BlindDate Communications, and Mary Ziegler, the artist's companion, for their help with this catalogue.

After its showing at the CAC, **Innuendo Non Troppo** travels to five other institutions nationwide. For their support of this exhibition and tour, we thank Townsend D. Wolfe, The Arkansas Arts Center, Little Rock; Daniel E. Stetson, Polk Museum of Art, Lakeland, Florida; Ted Potter, Anderson Gallery, Virginia Commonwealth University, Richmond; Sandy Harthorn, Boise Art Museum; and Cathy Kimball, San Jose Museum of Art.

Finally, we thank the artist for his vision and wondrous work. His efforts have opened our eyes to a new world.

Charles Desmarais, Director

The Scream (*work in progress*)

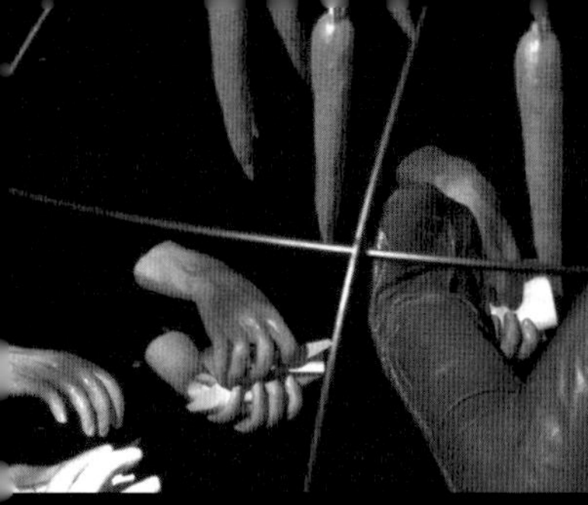

Leçon sur l'Herbe (work in progress)

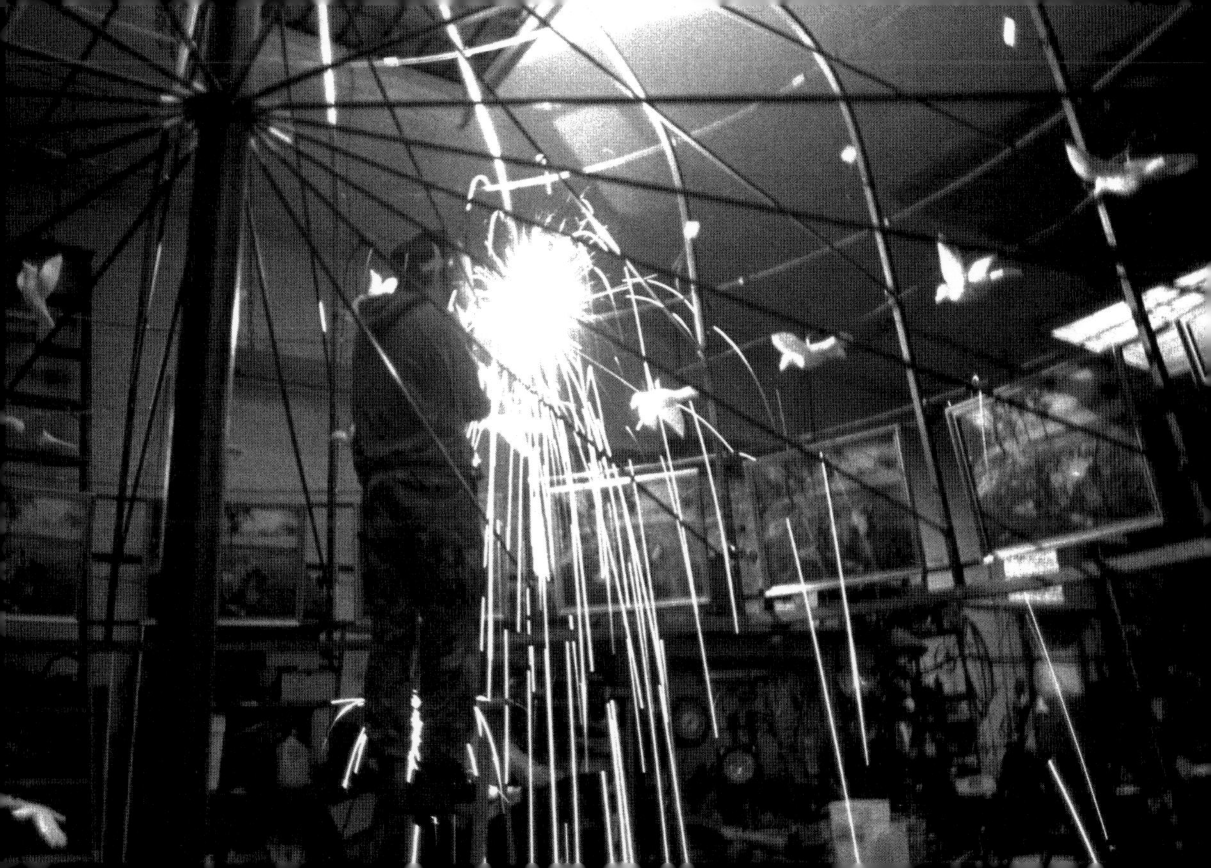

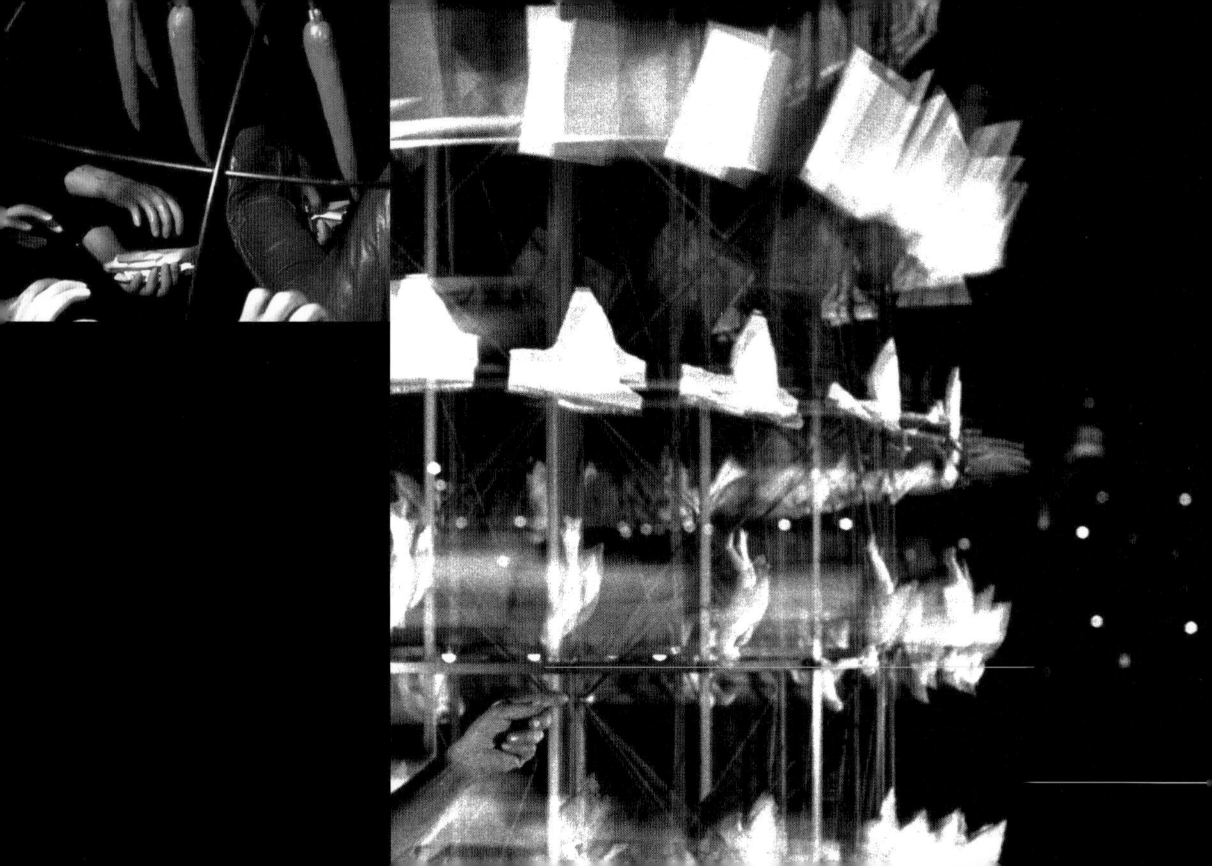

*You know the reason why some nights
you don't have a dream?
When there's just blackness?
And total silence?*

*Well, this is the reason:
It's because on that night
you are in somebody else's dream.
And this is the reason you can't
be in your own dream because
you're already busy
in somebody else's dream.*

Laurie Anderson

Transfiguration (detail), 1996
Collection Tempozan Gendaikan Contemporary Museum, Osaka, Japan

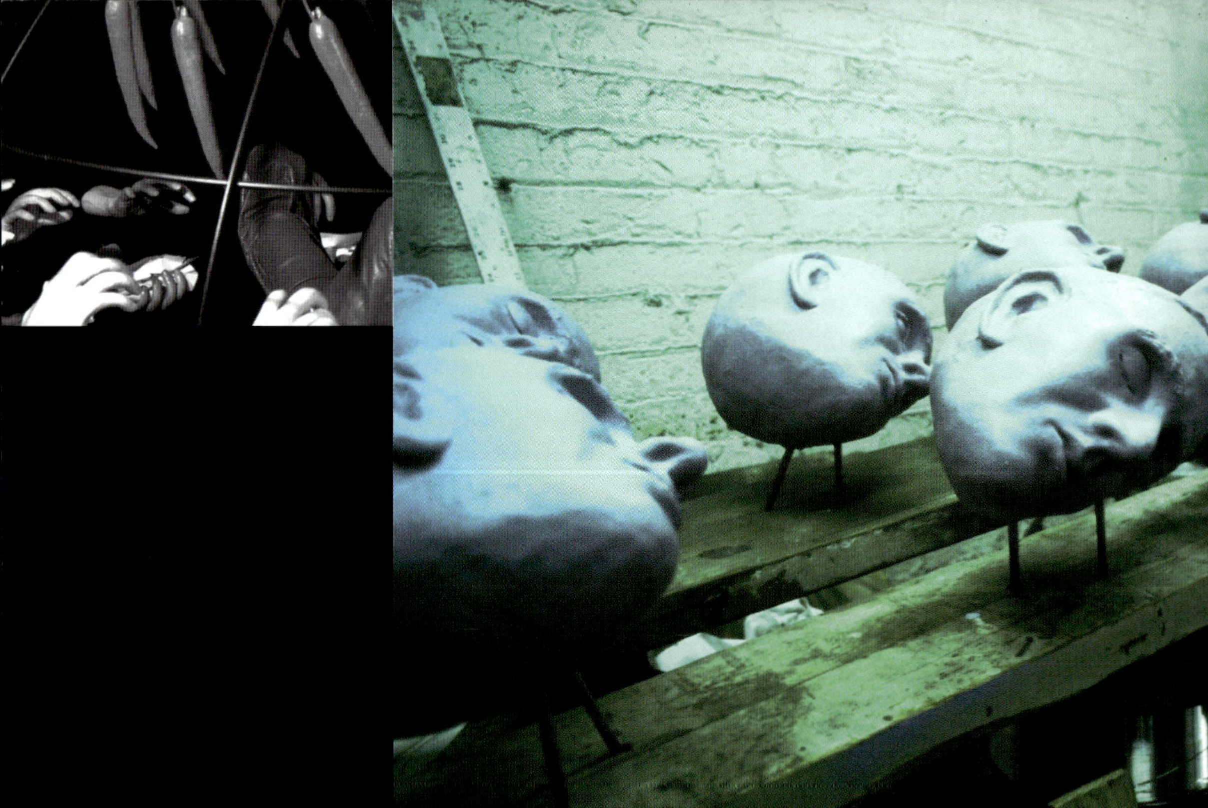

Disturbing the Waking State: an essay by David J. Brown

The first thing you notice is a whirring in the darkness. The humming of electricity flowing through gears, shafts, sealed bearings and steel rods. Then the tic-tic-ticking of lights, some thirteen times a second. The lights conjure up before you a hallucinogenic array of transformations: trucks running amok inside a cake; tumbling glasses spilling photographs; lizards being scooped from the pages of a book.

Gregory Barsamian builds machines that produce three-dimensional animation. According to the artist, "What I end up doing is mounting three dimensional, sequentially formed artworks on a motorized rotating cylinder. The cylinder is divided into segments like a piece of pie, in the neighborhood of sixteen frames. A strobe light is synchronized to flash as each frame passes. Each frame becomes like a single image in a film composed of and slightly different from the preceding and following frames. That's how I create the movement."

Die Falle (*work in progress*)

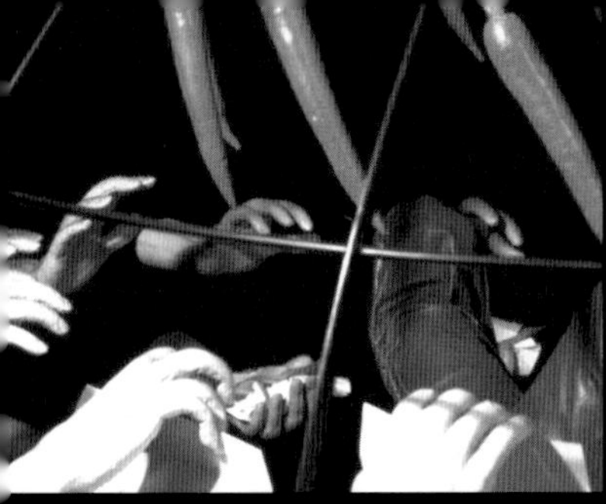

Putti (detail), 1991
Courtesy the artist and Schmidt Bingham Gallery

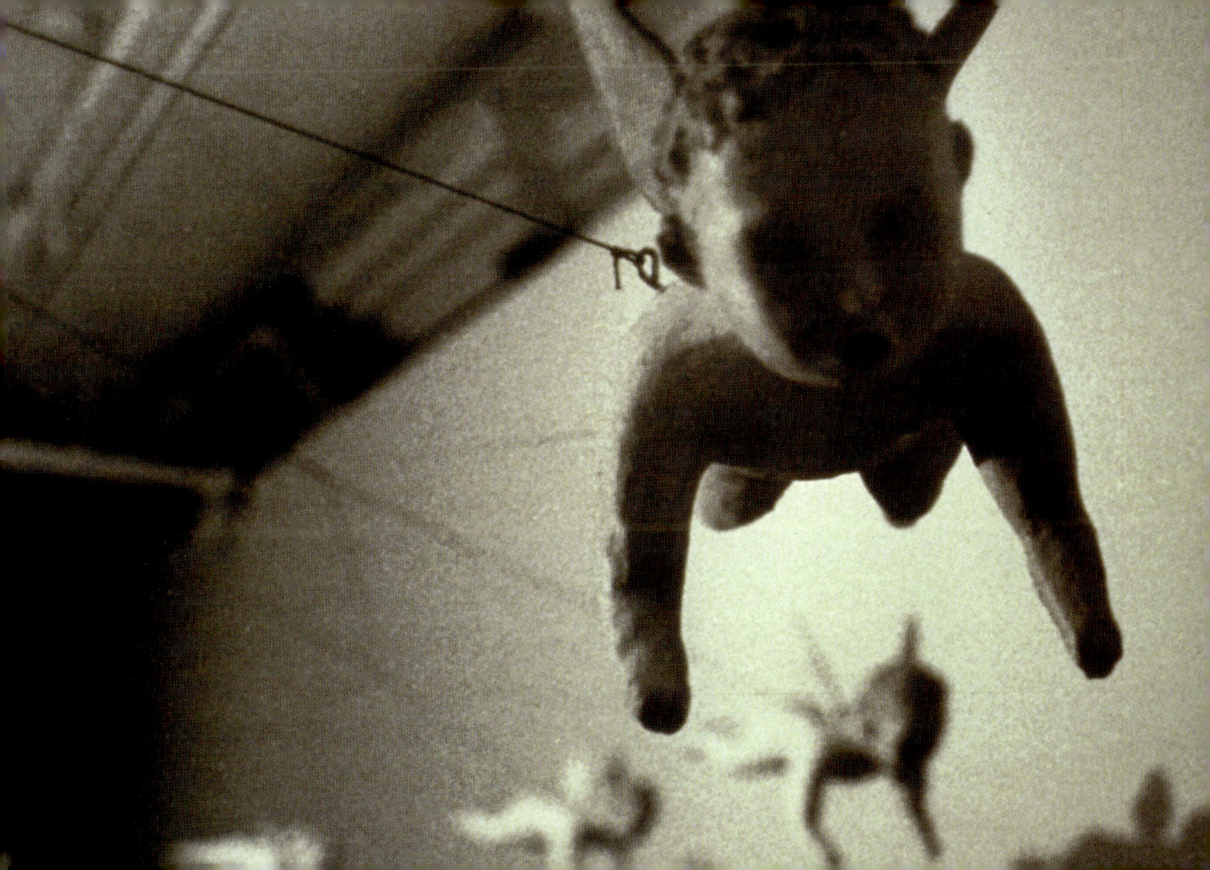

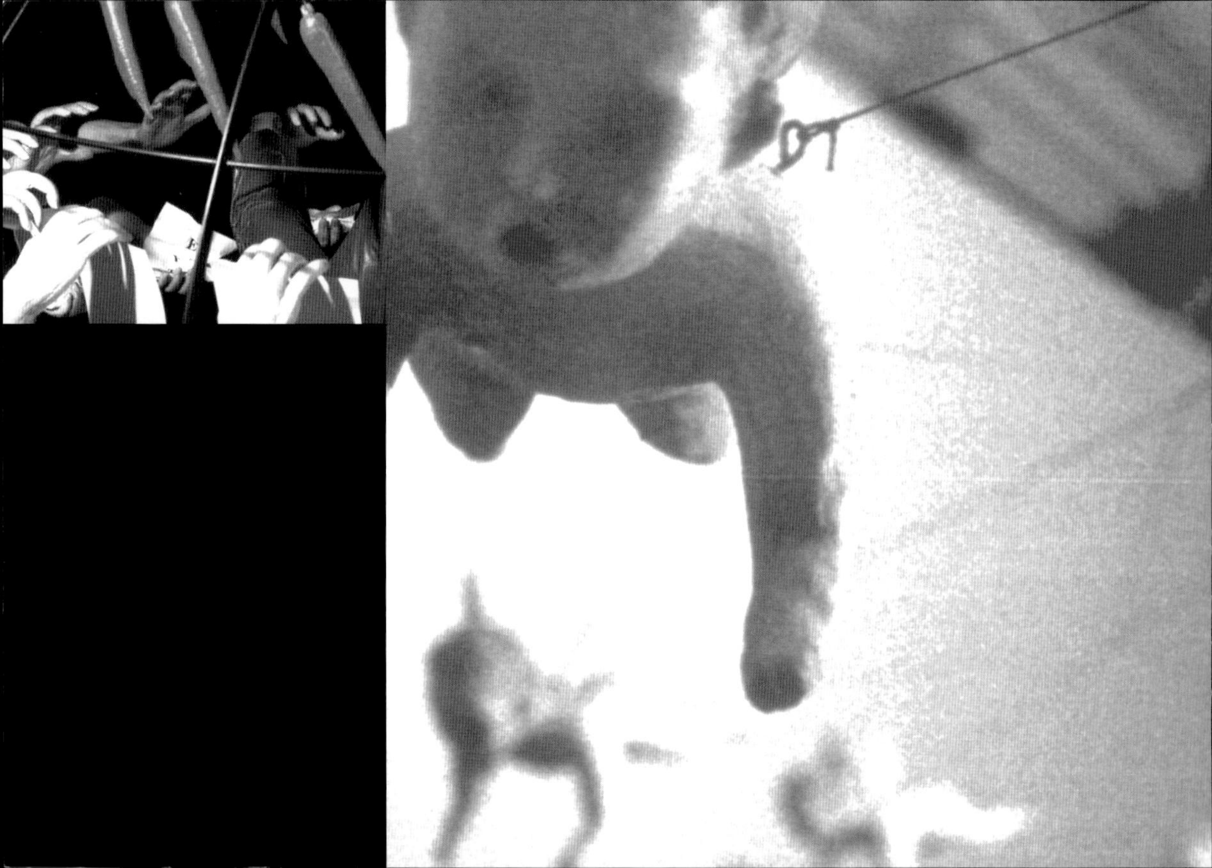

The machinery is used to create stories that we only dream about—complicated, powerful, ethereal. For the past fifteen years, the artist has recorded the seemingly random and often disjointed images of his dreams. He has gotten so proficient at it that he can roll over, switch on a recorder, and describe the actions that are taking place, often without waking. "At times, if I don't disturb myself too much, I'll actually fall back asleep and record it as it's happening—all sorts of strange things can happen that way," says Barsamian. "After a while, listening to these tapes, you can actually begin to speak the language of dreams. You understand the language and can fabricate sequences in the language that you may not have had a specific dream of."

These dream sequences provide the point of departure for the philosophical questions that Barsamian tackles—many dealing with the universal nature of our existence: Are we, as individuals, in control of our own destiny? What factors exist that may interfere with the progression of intellect and

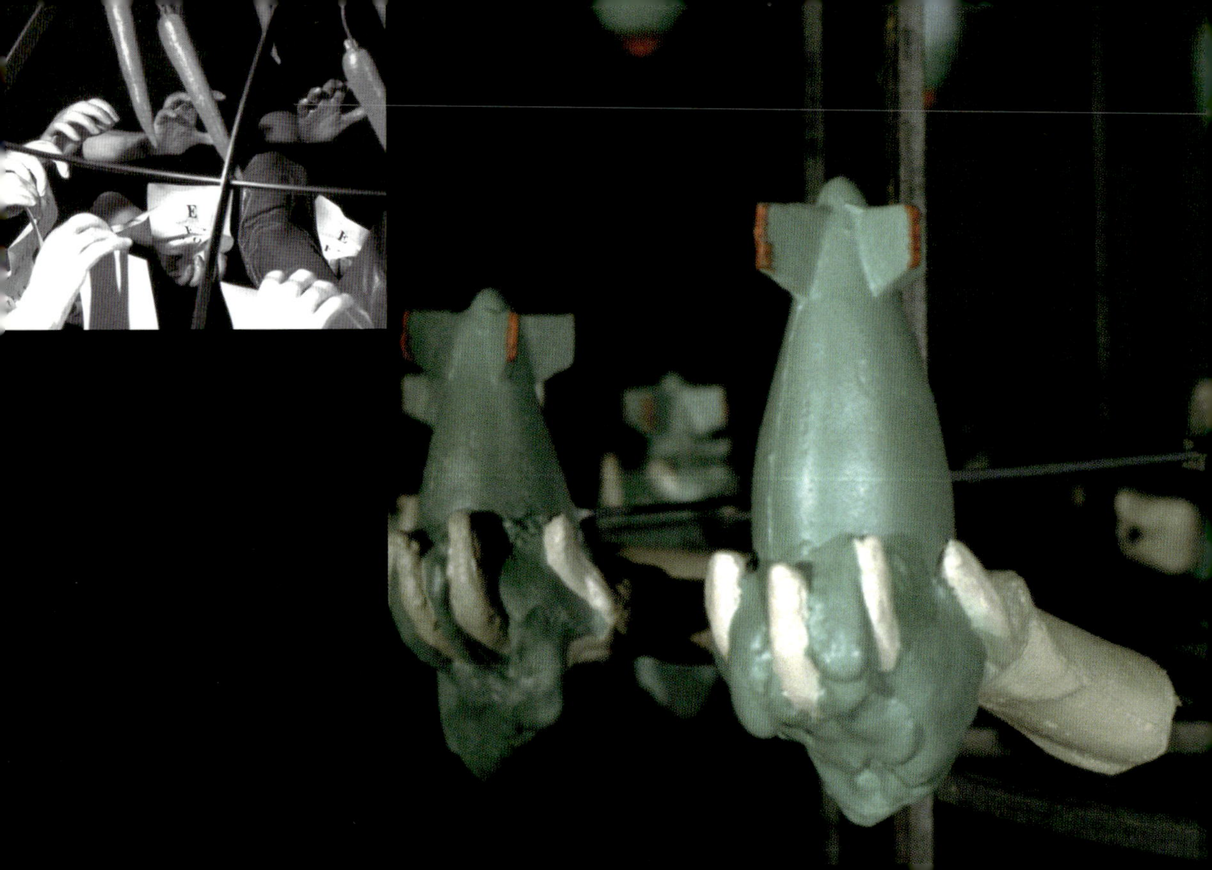

will? And what role does the subconscious play in coping with life in this technological age?

"Our world, when viewed from any one angle, is incomplete and when viewed from all angles, is incoherent. No single perspective takes into account the infinite variations in our experience."

The artist's early experiences shaped much of his work. Barsamian describes his youth as "typical," having grown up in Skokie, Illinois, a suburb of Chicago. His father amassed a collection of old automobiles, working on them as a hobby. That interest in cars and mechanics was passed from father to son, and is still very visible in the artist's work. "If you know a car, you know most machinery and their assembly techniques," remarks the artist.

Barsamian spent nine years at the University of Wisconsin in Madison, where he majored in philosophy, enrolled in a variety of art classes, and

Feral Fount (detail), 1996
Collection American Museum of the Moving Image, Astoria, NY

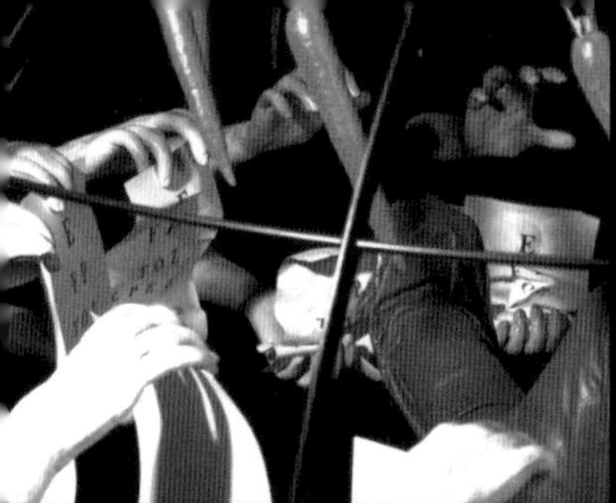

Dishwatcher, 1988
Courtesy the artist and Schmidt Bingham Gallery

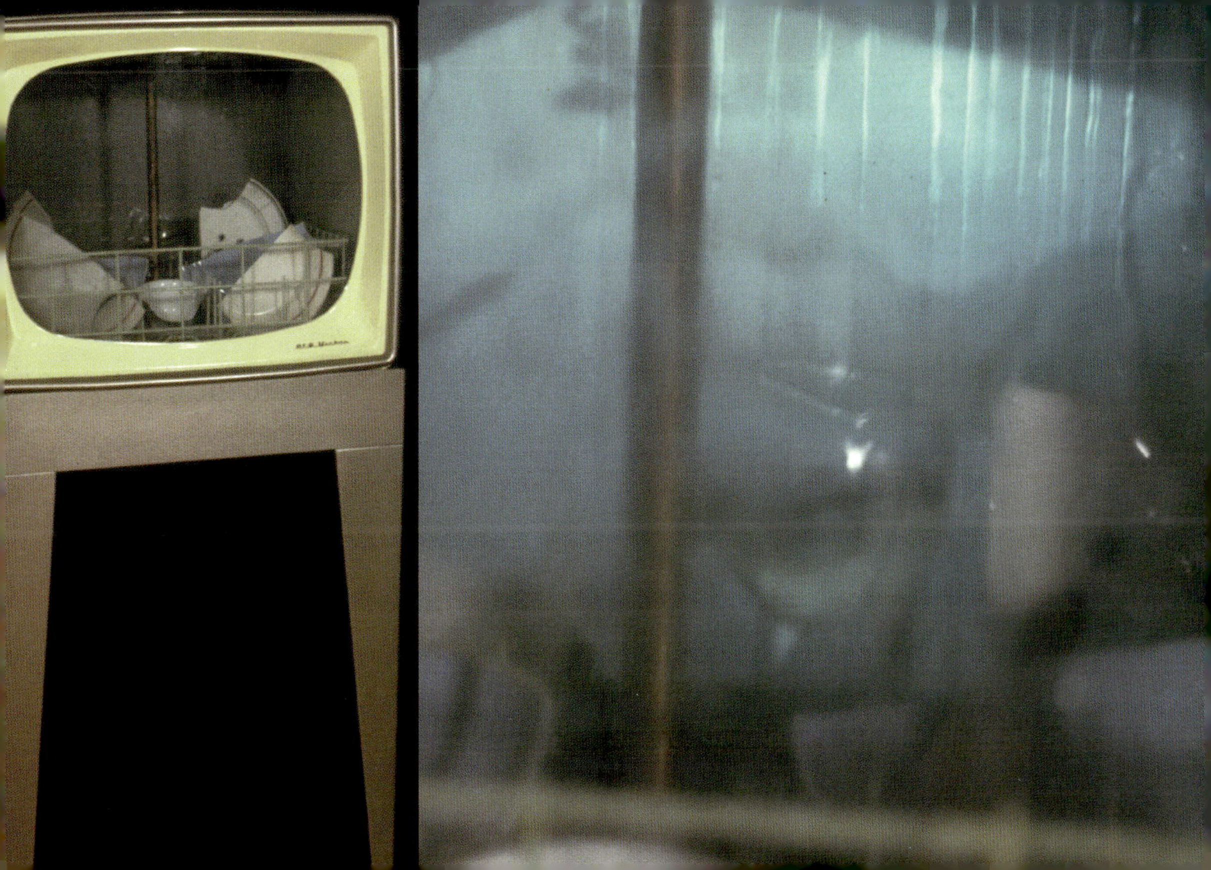

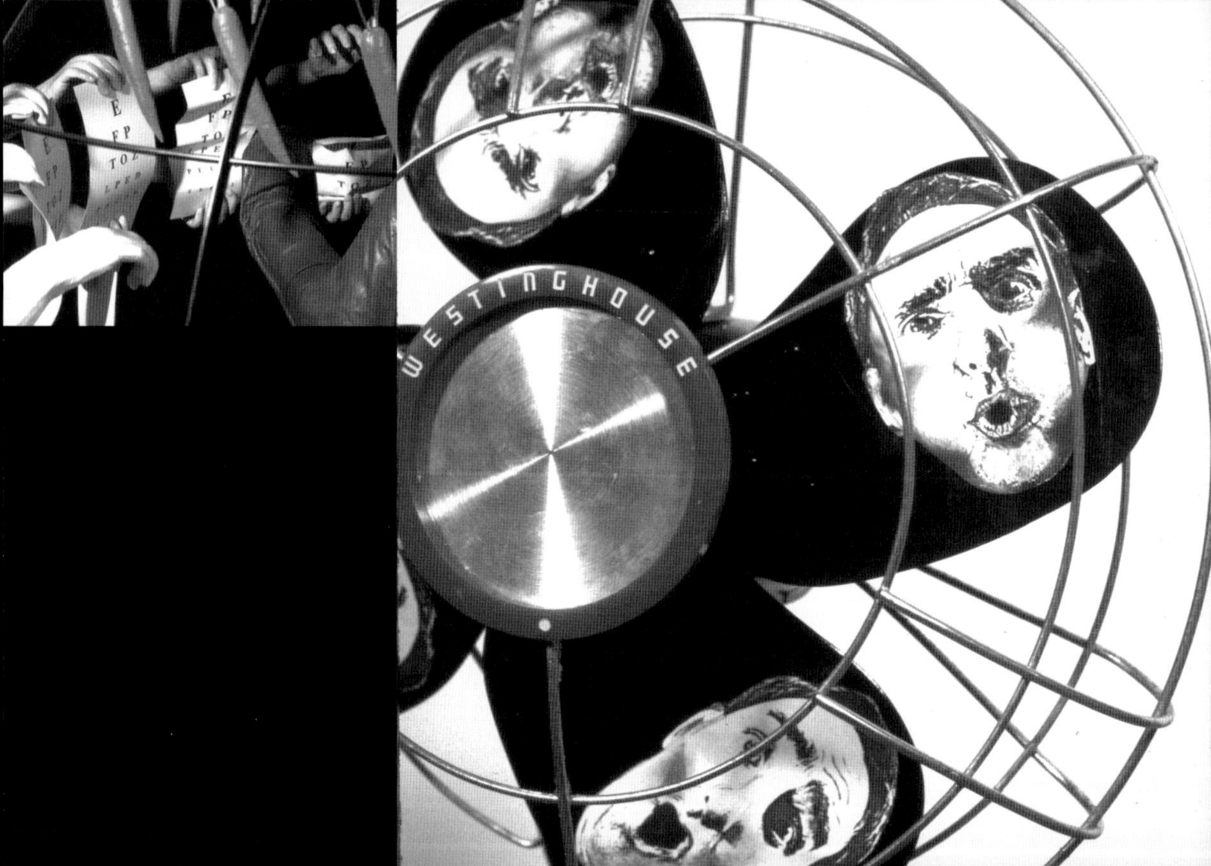

WESTINGHOUSE
E
FP
TOZ
LPED

worked part-time at a bicycle shop. Barsamian cites the work of the nineteenth-century philosopher Freidrich Nietzsche and the investigations of
the subconscious by the twentieth-century psychiatrist Carl Jung as major
influences at that time.

Moving to New York in the early 1980s, Barsamian purchased an old
building in the Williamsburg area of Brooklyn. "I spent the next four
years renovating it into a studio and several apartments. The effort provided enough financial security that I could pursue my artwork without
having to worry about being evicted or having to support a large rent," he
says. Works from that period include **Dishwatcher** (1988), which the
artist describes as an altered appliance meant to appease the suburban
mentality. His large ground-floor studio overflows with his reworking of
industrial-sized tools and appliances found in the streets and alleys of the
once heavy-industrial community.

Seeking to combine his diverse interests and skills, Barsamian became

Fan (detail), 1988
Private collection

Night of the Audile, 1991 (following two pages)
Collection Musée Chateau, Annecy, France

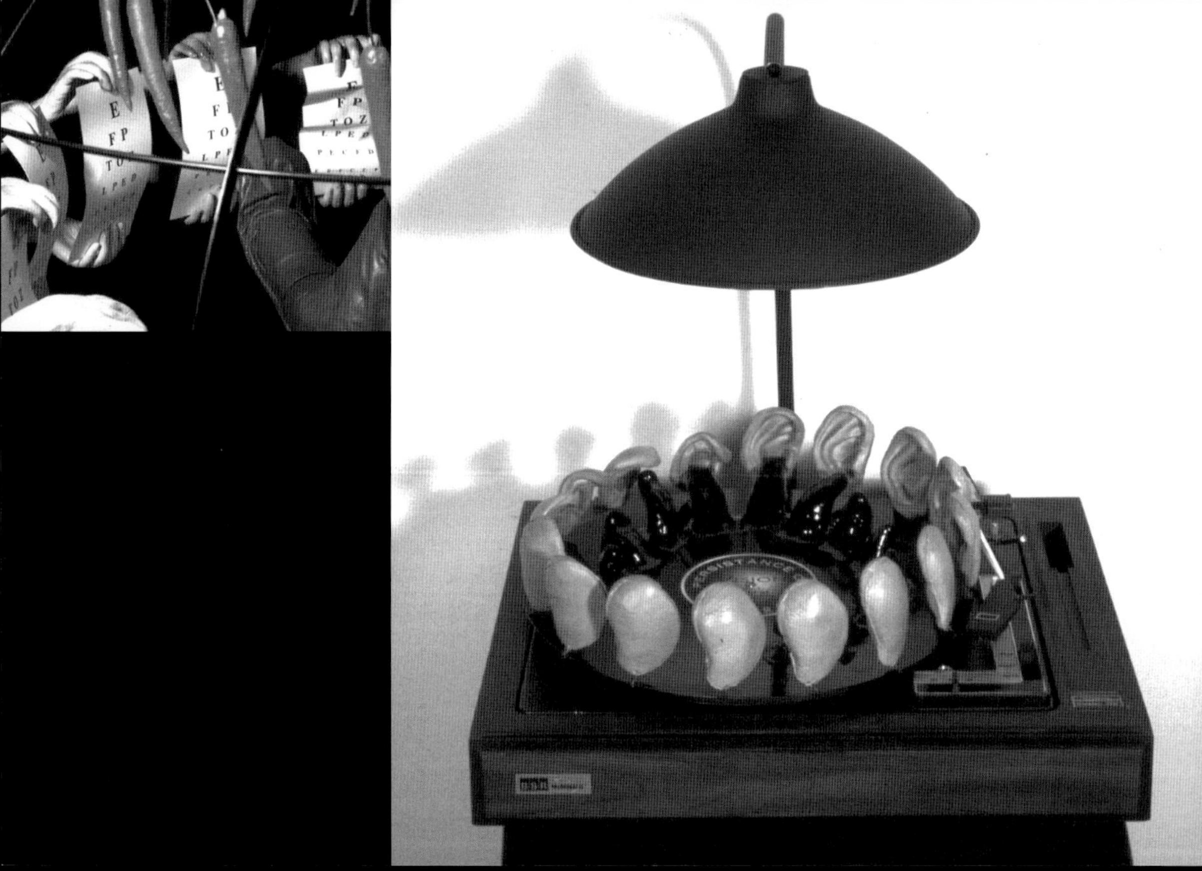

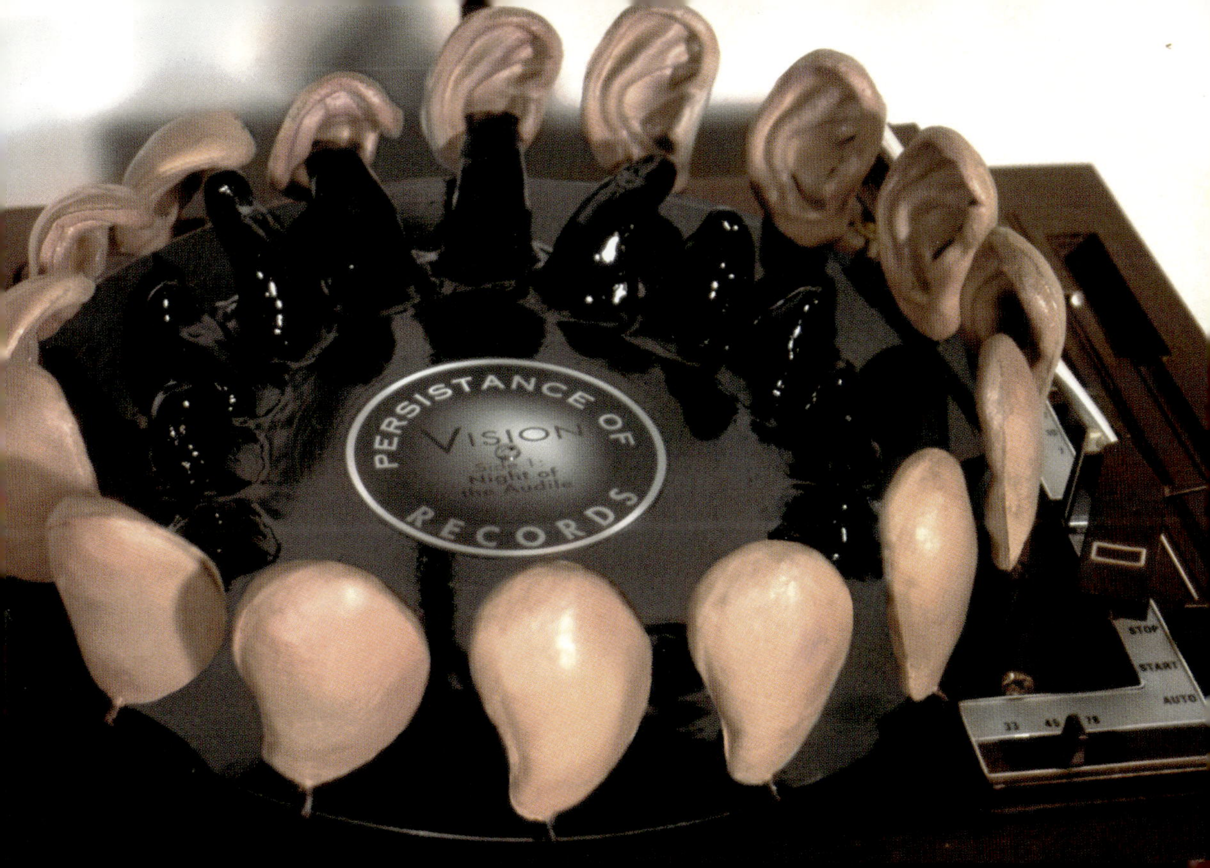

PERSISTANCE OF RECORDS
VISION
Side 1:
Night of
the Audile
STOP
START
AUTO
33 45 78

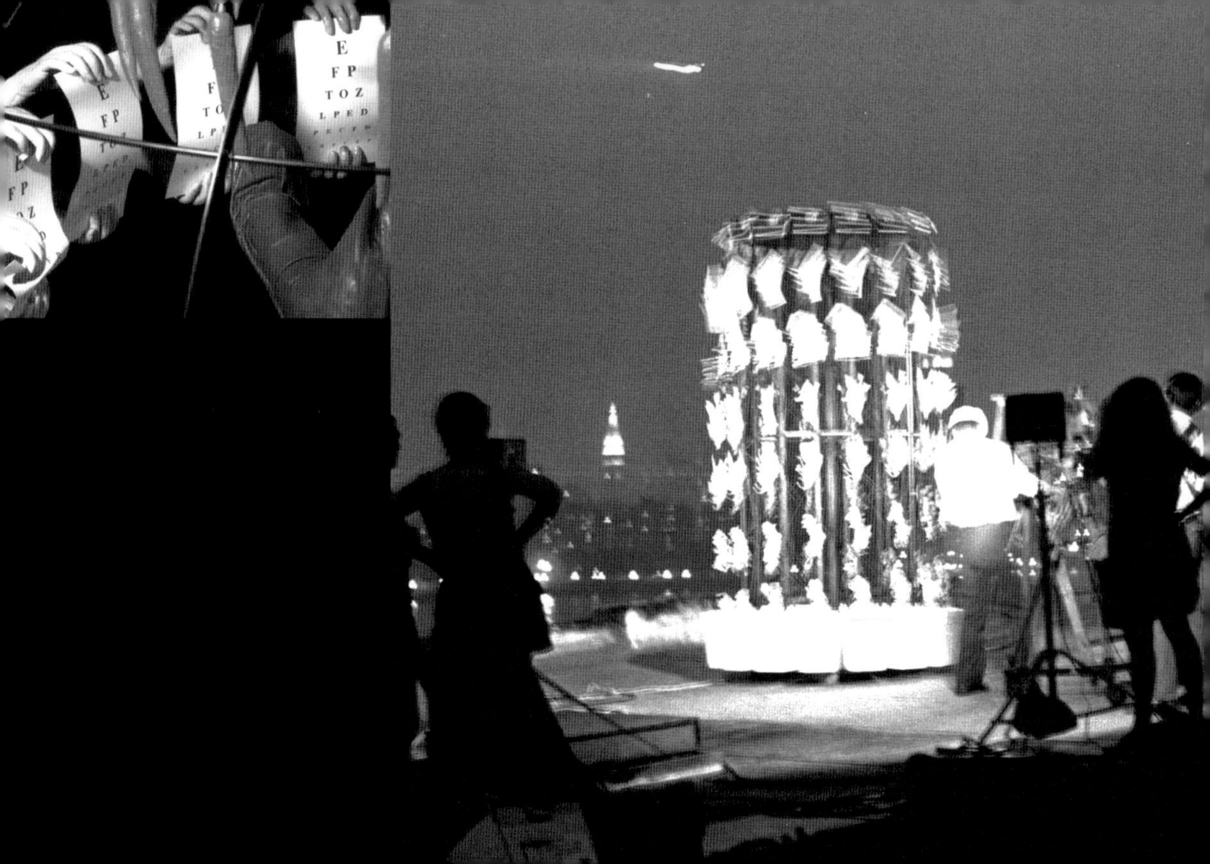

fascinated with the possibilities of animation. "Animation is an ideal medium for dream imagery," says the artist. "It allows a person to create metamorphosis in real time–things that are impossible in real life."

The low-tech zoetrope, invented by William George Horner in 1834, became the starting point. This optical device and parlor toy consists of a slot-pierced drum of metal, open at the top, that revolves on a pivot attached to a heavy base. Inside the drum are bands of paper equal in length to the circumference of the drum. On the paper appear figures and images in various states of movement, painted in flat colors. When viewed through one of the slots as the drum is manually rotated, the figures appear to move. "The zoetrope was developed over 150 years ago and was the ancestor of modern cinema. It relied on the principle of persistence of vision, whereby an image flashed before the eye is retained until the next one comes along. The brain knits them into a coherent whole, just as frames in a film pass by one by one into a fluid movement. The earliest

Japanese film crew on roof of artist's studio, Brooklyn, NY

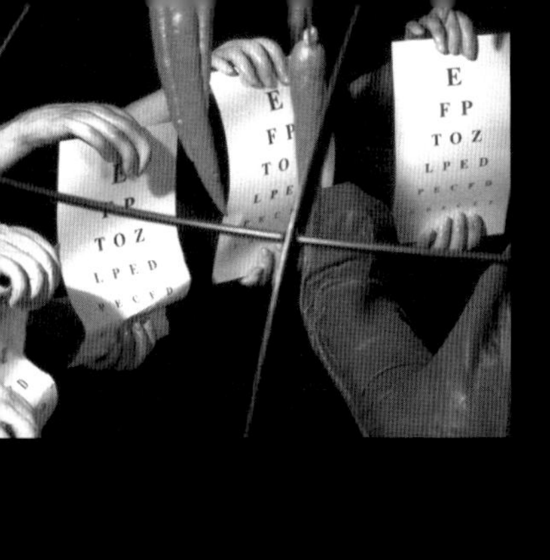

optical devices involved a succession of images which, when viewed through a shutter, animated those images into a sequence," describes Barsamian. "In the beginning, I was just playing with the concept. I knew basically how it could work and I took some super-8 film footage of a friend walking and projected them frame by frame onto a piece of paper tacked to the wall. I traced his image and made cutouts of his body in the walking motion. I then took these cutouts and mounted them on a wheel, synchronized a strobe light to it and sure enough, the paper cutouts walked. It was at that moment that it dawned on me that they didn't have to be two-dimensional. I could animate wholly three-dimensional objects."

• • •

"Cross-over artist" is a phrase generally used in the music business, yet it seems appropriate when describing Barsamian's work. Between 1994 and 1997, the artist produced a series of large-scale commissions for institutions as varied as science centers and art museums. Curators at one type

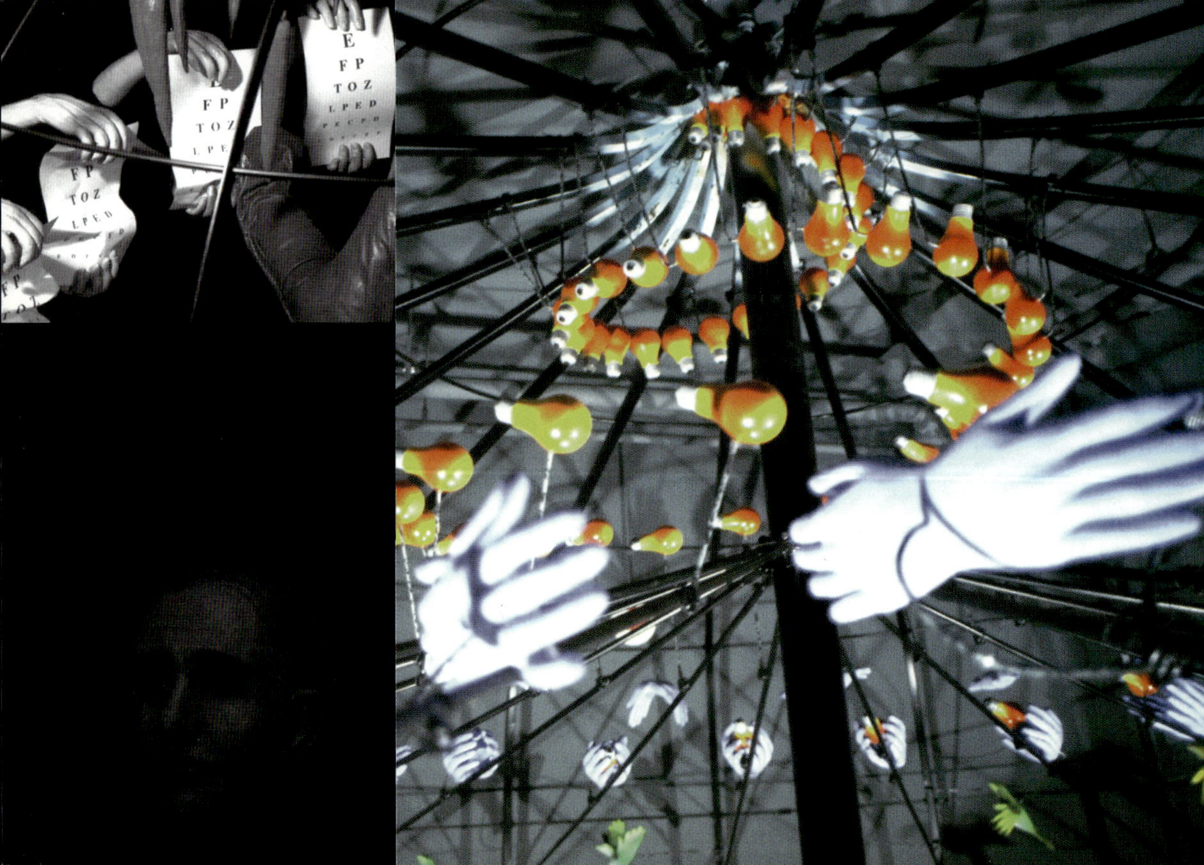

of institution respond to the unique cinematic quality of the mechanical works, while others applaud his careful incorporation of universal images. Commingled with this imagery and mechanics are Barsamian's profound and quizzical probings. It is misleading, however, that the artist has been invited to exhibit at such venues as the Nippon Telegraph and Telephone's InterCommunication Center, a state-of-the-art technology museum in Tokyo. With the exception of Barsamian's work **Juggler** (1997), all of the ICC-commissioned pieces, from artists around the world, are computer-based or computer-driven.

Barsamian's sculptures are the opposite of high-tech, owing more to the nineteenth-century's idea of vision. In the early nineteenth-century a succession of scientific discoveries radically challenged the Renaissance invention of perspective, overturning the belief that vision is monocular-based. Vision was then discussed as a combination of external stimuli and physiological processes involving various functions of the body. Today,

Leçon sur l'Herbe (detail), 1994-1995
Collection Creative Discovery Museum, Chattanooga, TN

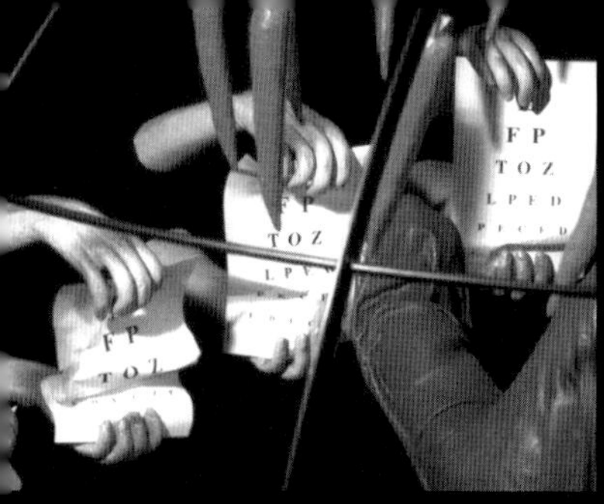
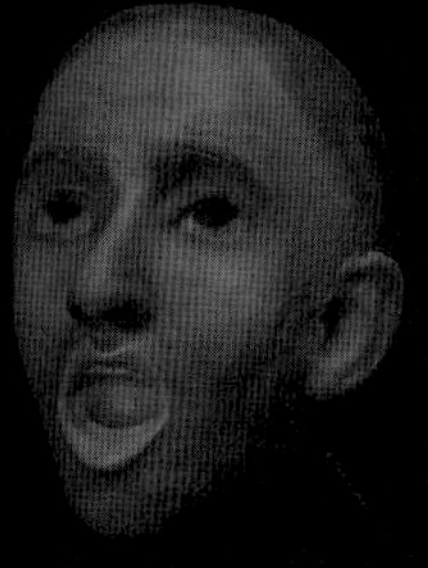

Juggler (details), 1986
Collection Nippon InterCommunication Center, Tokyo, Japan

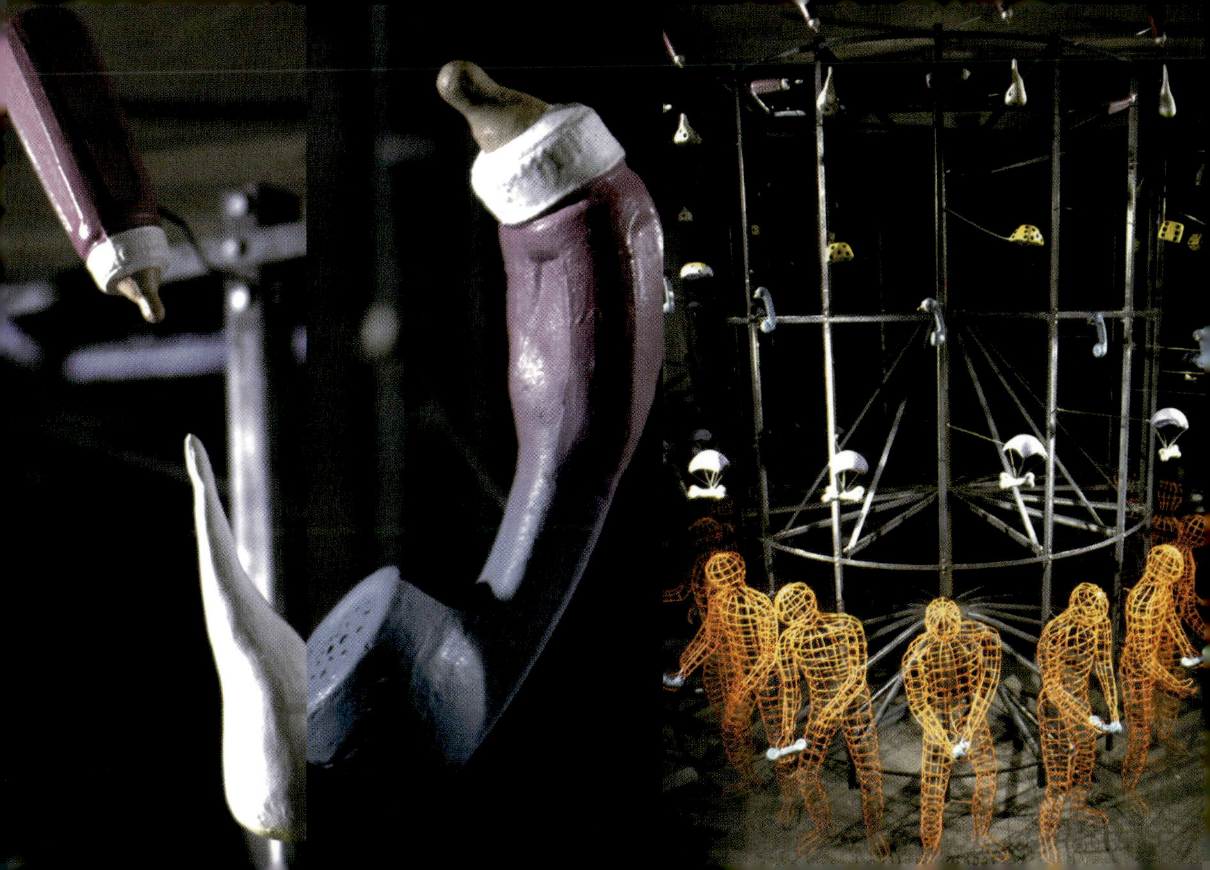

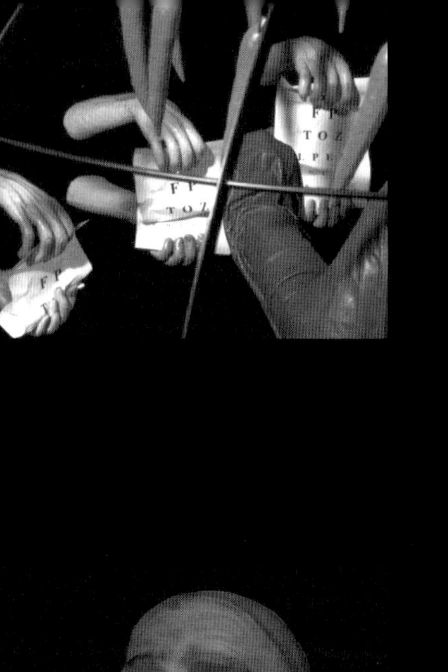
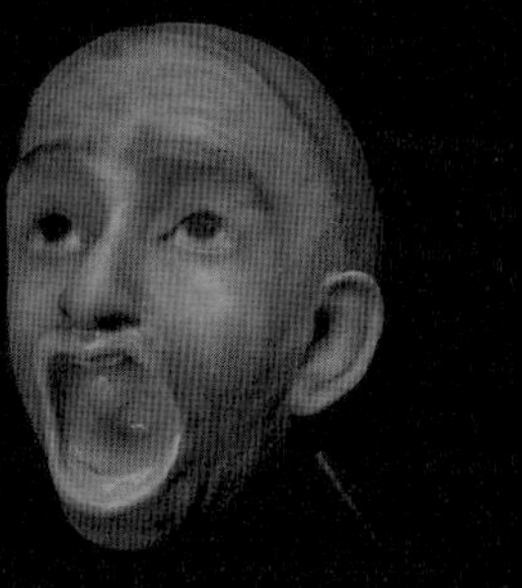

those revolutionary ideas regarding vision and perception are being challenged by the computer and its ramifications.

According to art historian Jonathan Crary, "Most of the historically important functions of the human eye are being supplanted by practices in which visual images no longer have any reference to the position of an observer in a 'real,' optically-perceived world. If these images can be said to refer to anything, it is to millions of bits of electronic mathematical data. Increasingly, visuality will be situated on a cybernetic and electromagnetic terrain where abstract and linguistic elements coincide and are consumed, circulated, and exchanged globally."

It remains to be seen whether Barsamian will incorporate the computer in future works. For now, he remains steadfast to the machine age and the intersection where the subconscious mind meets the fabricated realities of the modern world. "Whenever you use subconscious imagery in a work and leave it as open-ended as I do, you get an enormous variety of inter-

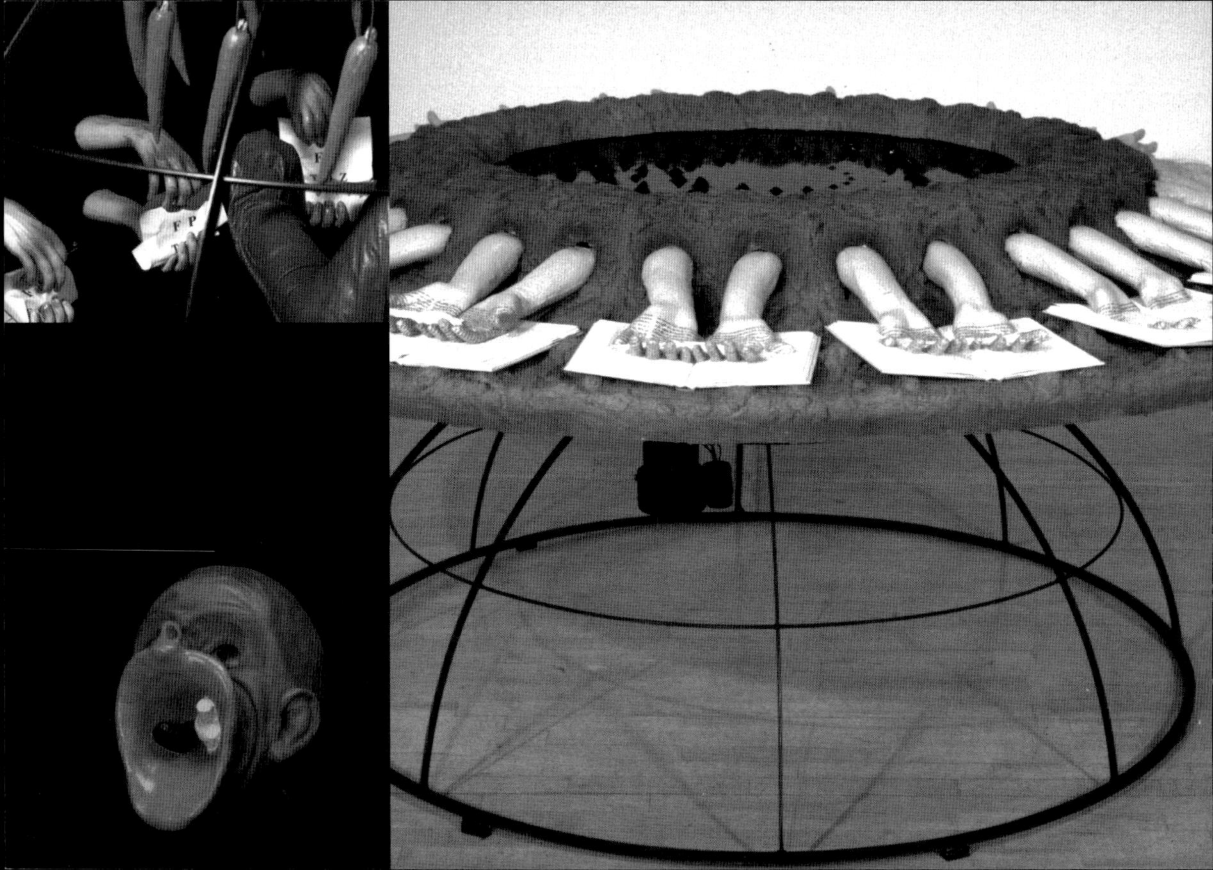

pretations. Rather than trying to control those interpretations, I am happy to witness them and enjoy them. You can't control them anyway. Once you create the imagery, it's up to the viewer to bring their own experience to it," states the artist.

Barsamian's earliest sculptures are simple in form, somewhat rugged in design, and illustrate the artist's wish to uncover the layers of illusion that we live under; that we attempt to differentiate ourselves from the natural world. This feeble attempt to distance ourselves from nature is, in Barsamian's view, a flaw in our genetic code. Consider **Dipping Digits (Always Gets Wet)**, a table-top-sized work from 1991. A mountainous wall surrounds a pool that the artist refers to as the primordial ooze, the basic biological origin of life, the center of it all. Protruding from the rock-form are sixteen sets of arms and hands. The hands dip into an open book filled with illegible text. As the hands rise, a lizard, also covered with text, slithers through their grasp. In discussing the work with the artist, several

Dipping Digits (Always Get Wet), 1991 (left and following two pages)
Courtesy the artist and Schmidt Bingham Gallery

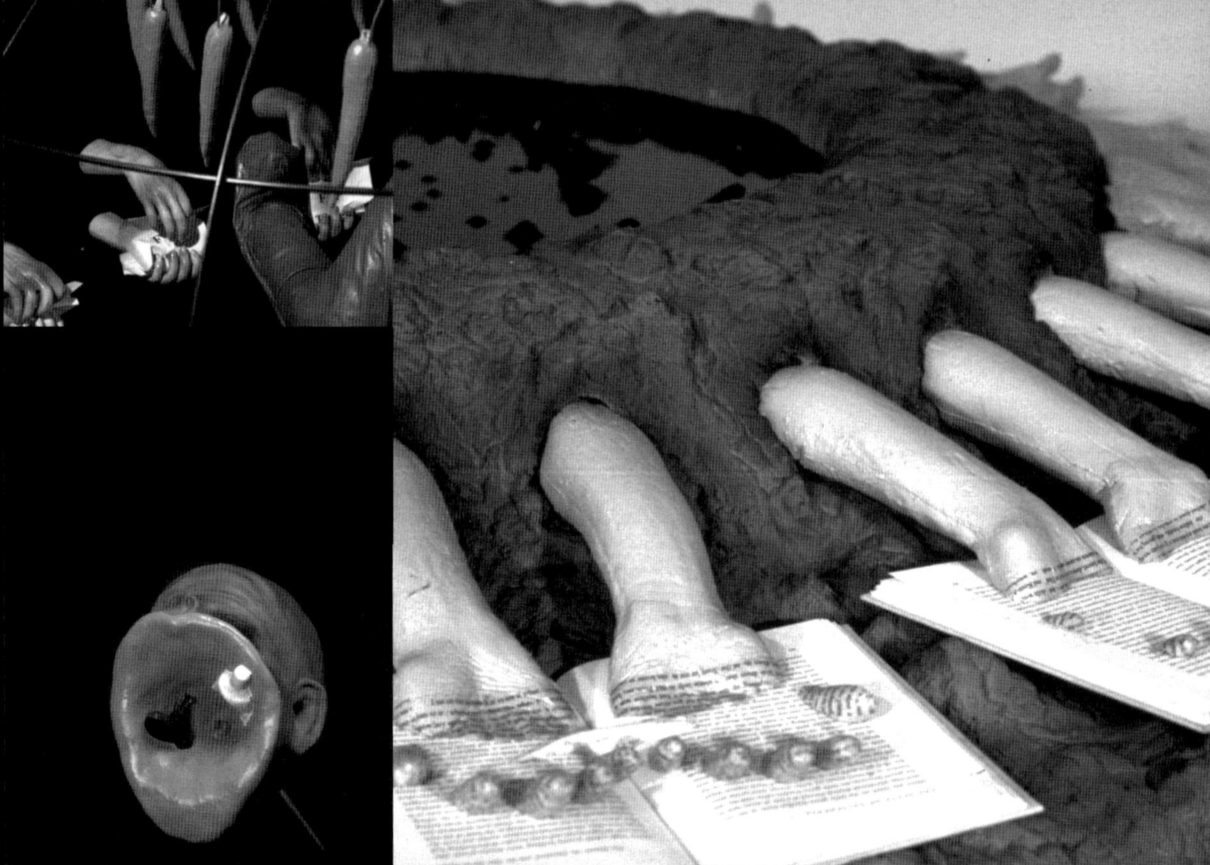

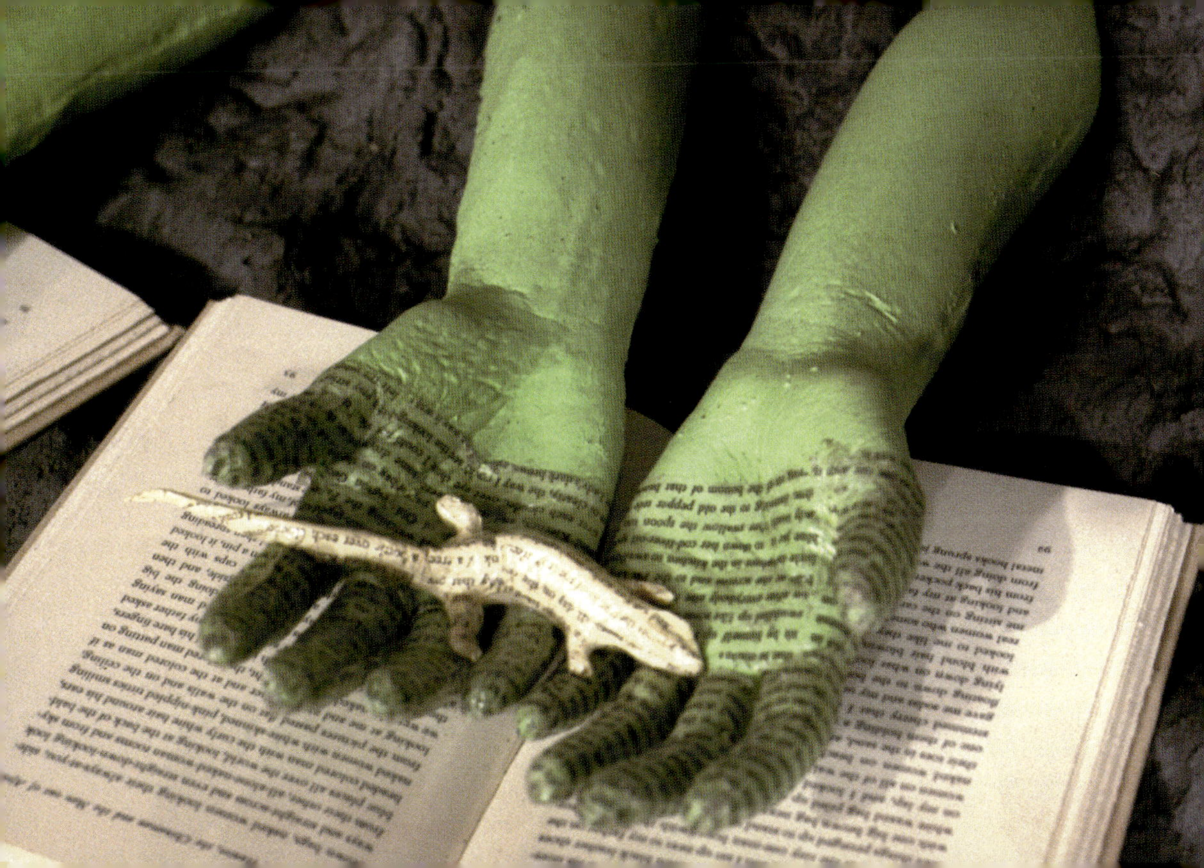

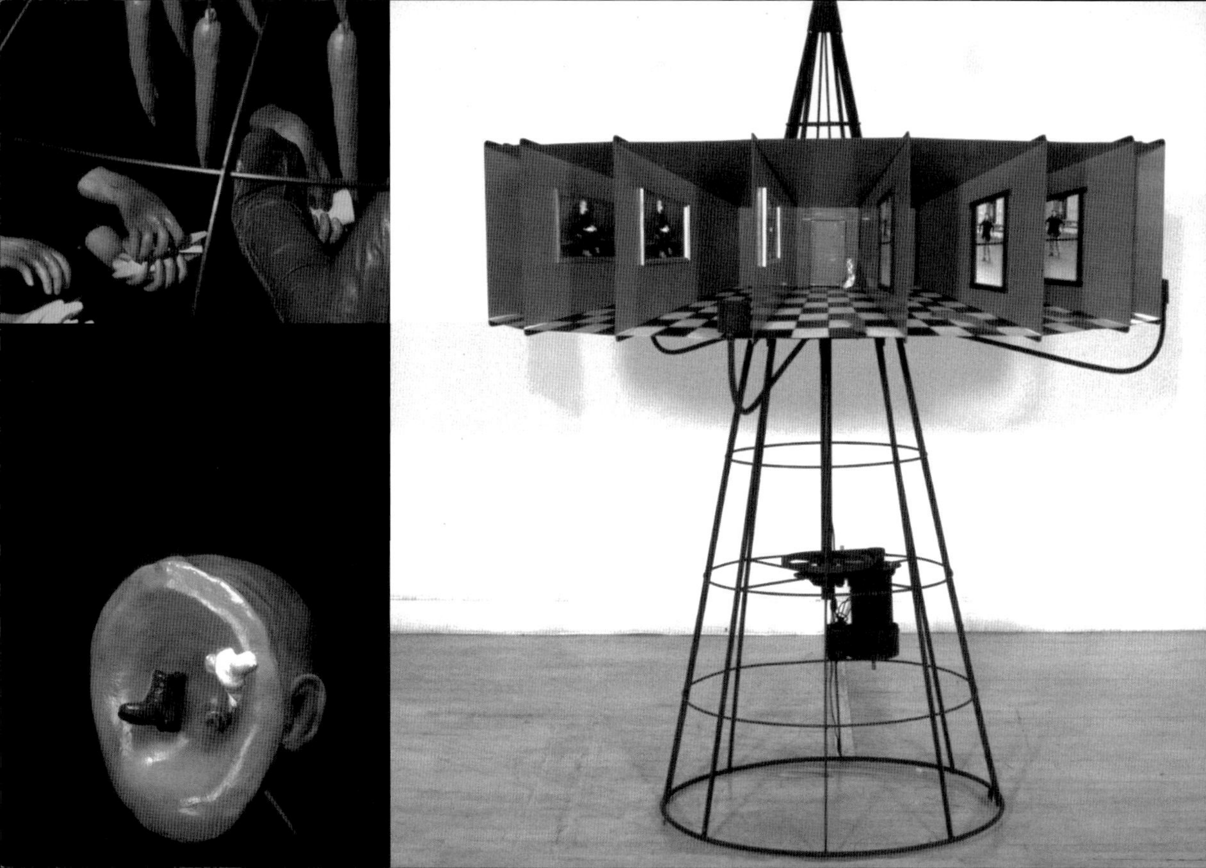

questions were raised: Is the range of our intellect designed to be limitless or has it already reached its capacity to process information? And does our quest for knowledge offer but a temporary respite from the limitations of our corporeal body?

Coprophagia (1991) is also a sculpture in the table-top format. The title, literally defined, refers to the eating of excrement. The work developed as a caustic response to the enticing display of high-tech weaponry and rah-rah reportage of the Gulf War on television sets across the United States. As Barsamian says, "I was hooked, fascinated, and disgusted that I was fascinated. I felt that I was being fed shit—eating it and liking it, but underneath disgusted."

We rely on all of our senses in perceiving the natural world. Can our response to this real world be subconsciously altered by technology? Sitting on his roof one night, Barsamian witnessed the movement of helicopters, landing and taking off at a nearby heliport. "They seemed like

Coprophagia, 1991   (left and following two pages)
Courtesy the artist and Schmidt Bingham Gallery

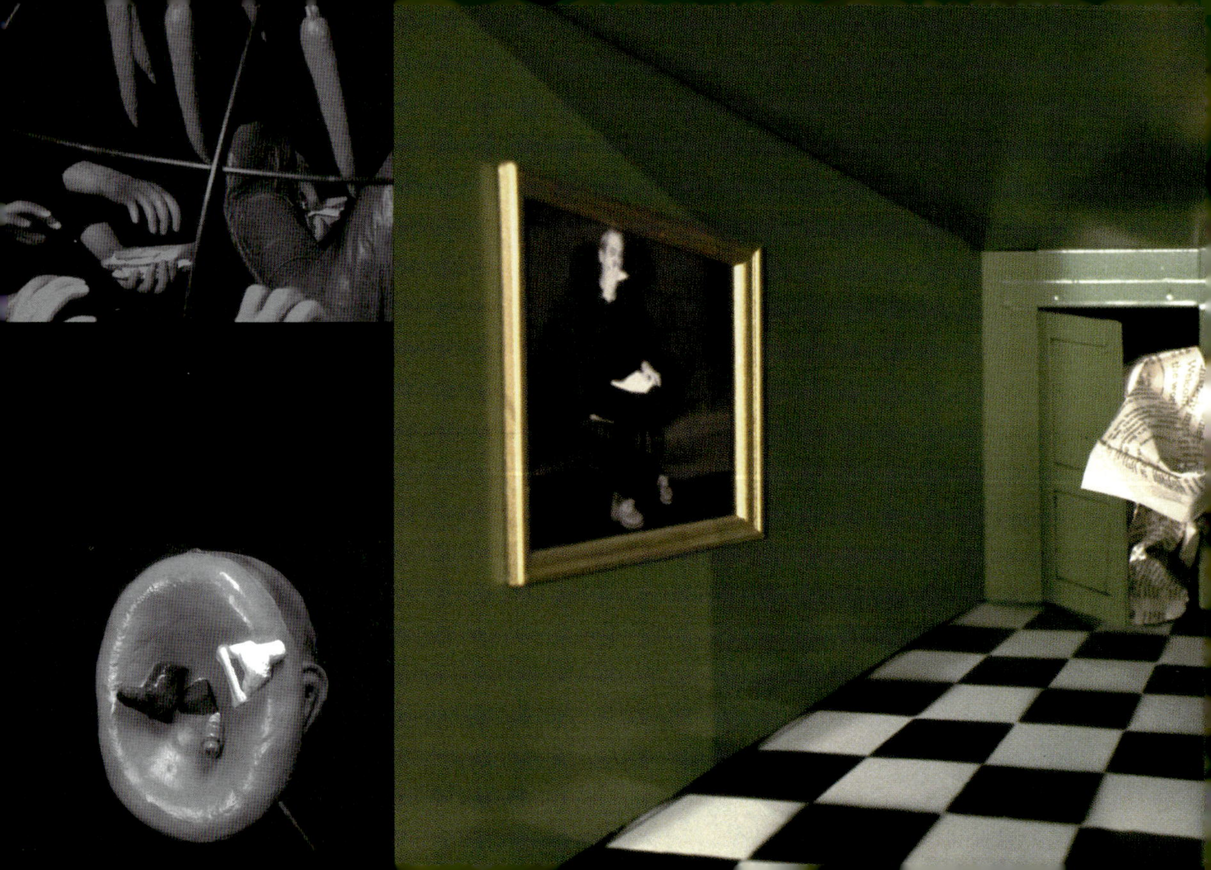

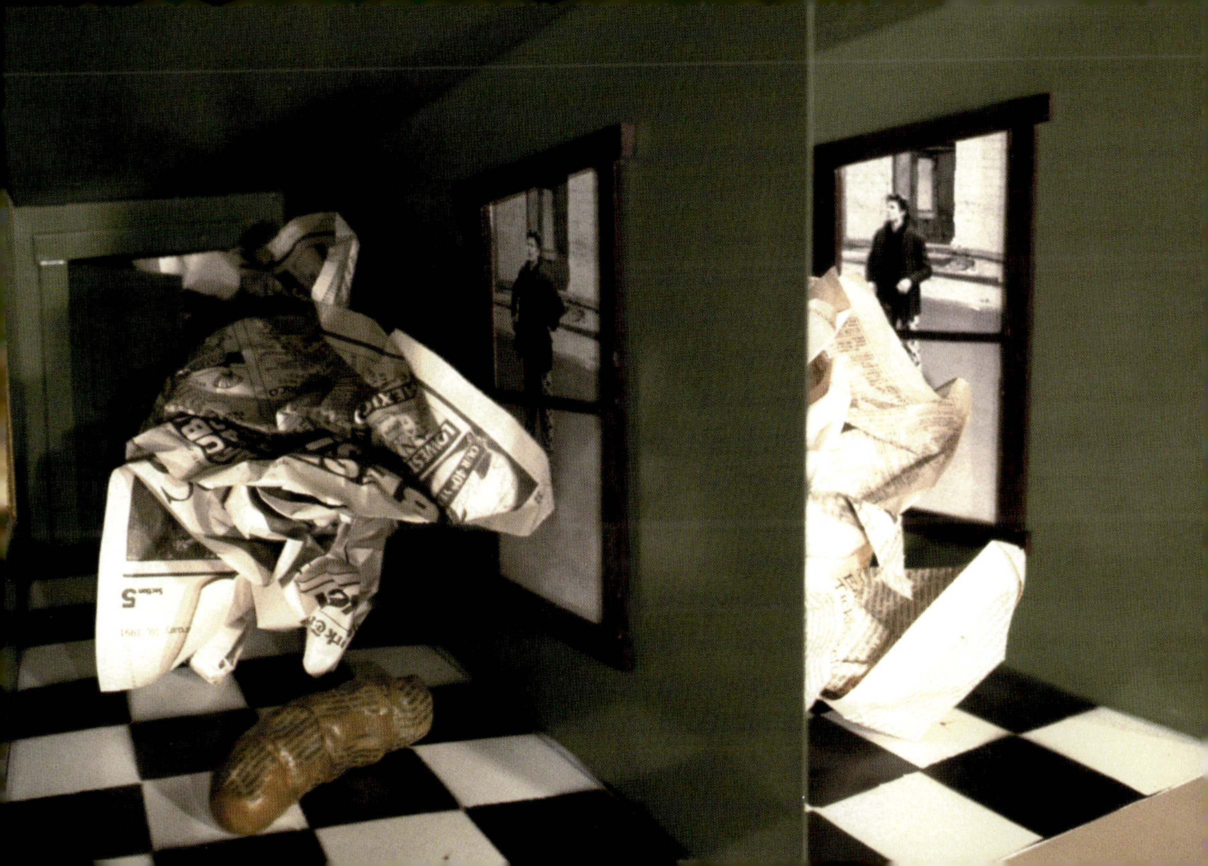

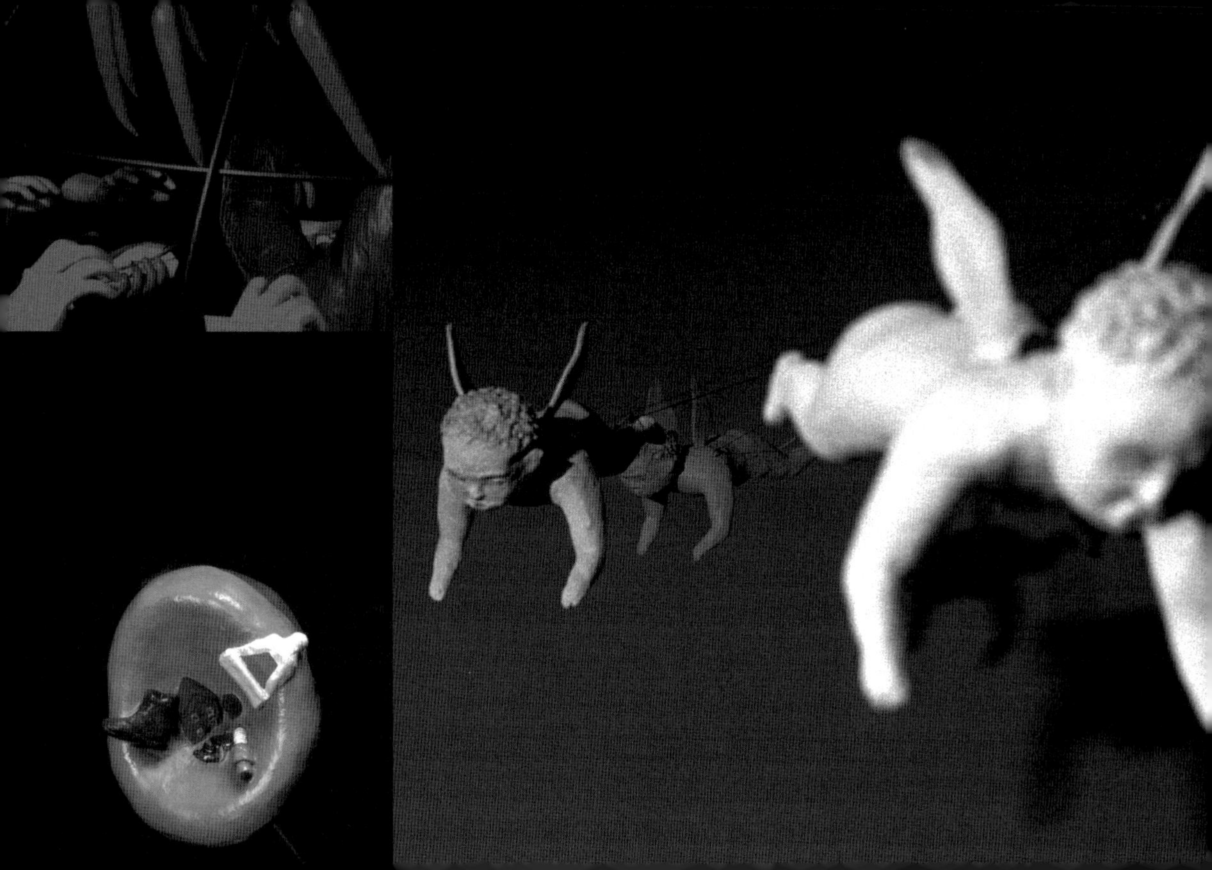

bees flying or angels attending the city," he says. The work **Putti** (1991) resulted from that experience and questions the validity of our perceptual responses. Spinning above your head and forming a large circle are sixteen shifting transformations. A cherub becomes a helicopter before changing back into itself in an endless Sysiphean arrangement. What seems at first to be the harbinger of joy becomes a much darker image, possibly some modern-day version of Jeremy Bentham's "Panopticon," a nineteenth-century plan for the ideal prison. Although never realized, the Panopticon was designed to create the threat of constant surveillance by never revealing the whereabouts of the observer. By making the observer invisible, Bentham's plan for the cultivation of paranoia could be used as a means of societal control.

The image of a birthday cake clearly symbolizes celebration. **Cake Walk** (1997) was inspired by a passage from Nietzche's *Also Sprach Zarathustra* that involves having the power of will to arrange the very moment of your

Putti (details), 1991 (left and following two pages)

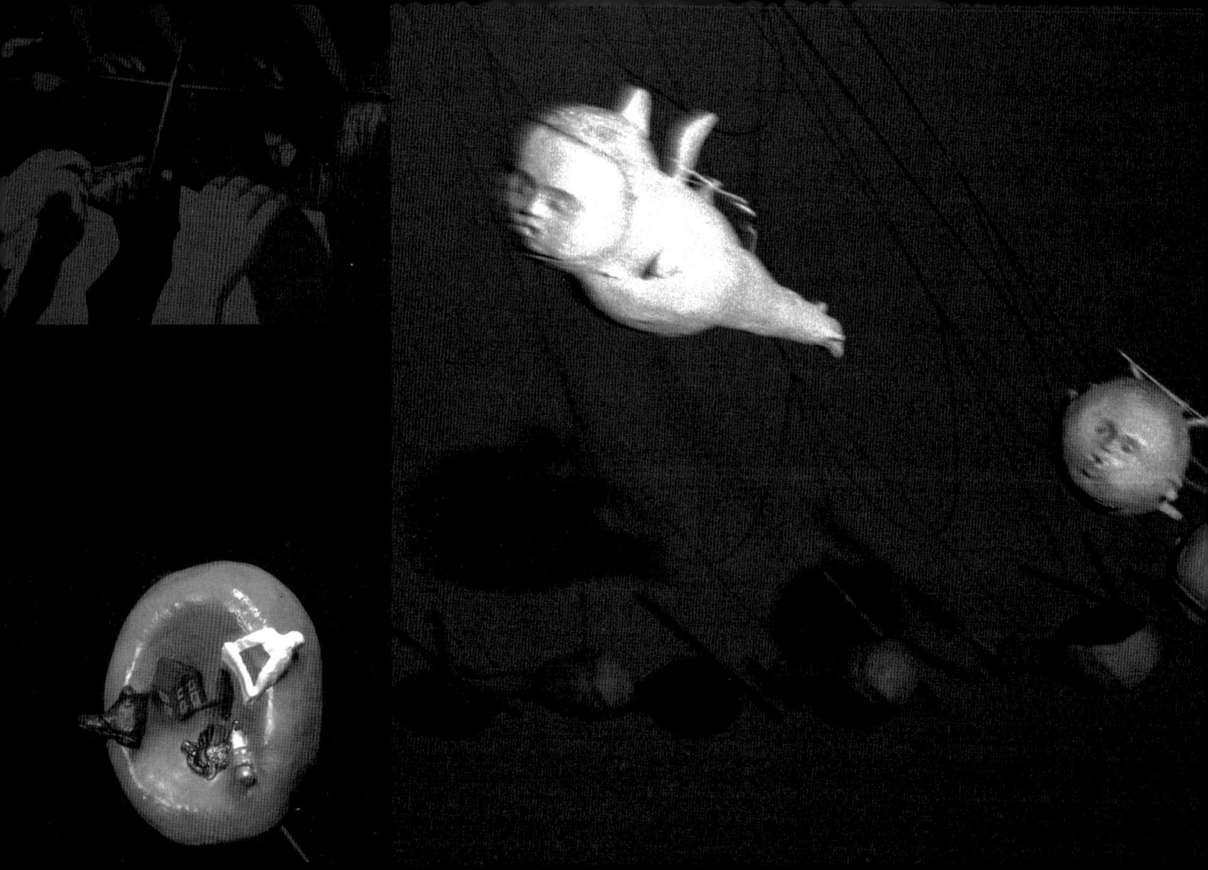

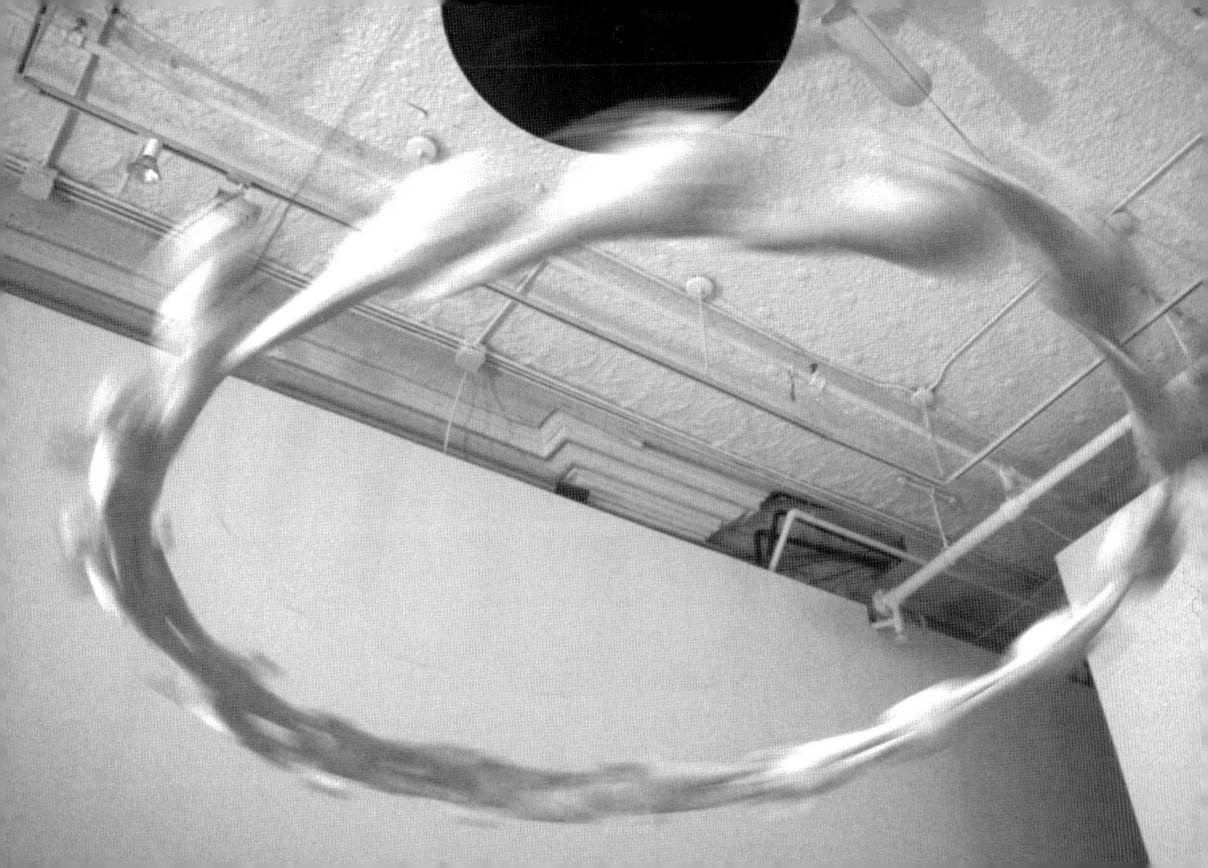

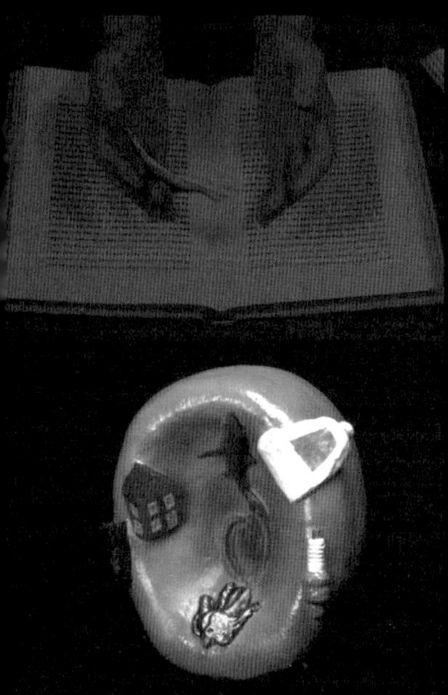

Cake Walk, *1997*
Collection Howard and Judy Tullman, Chicago, IL

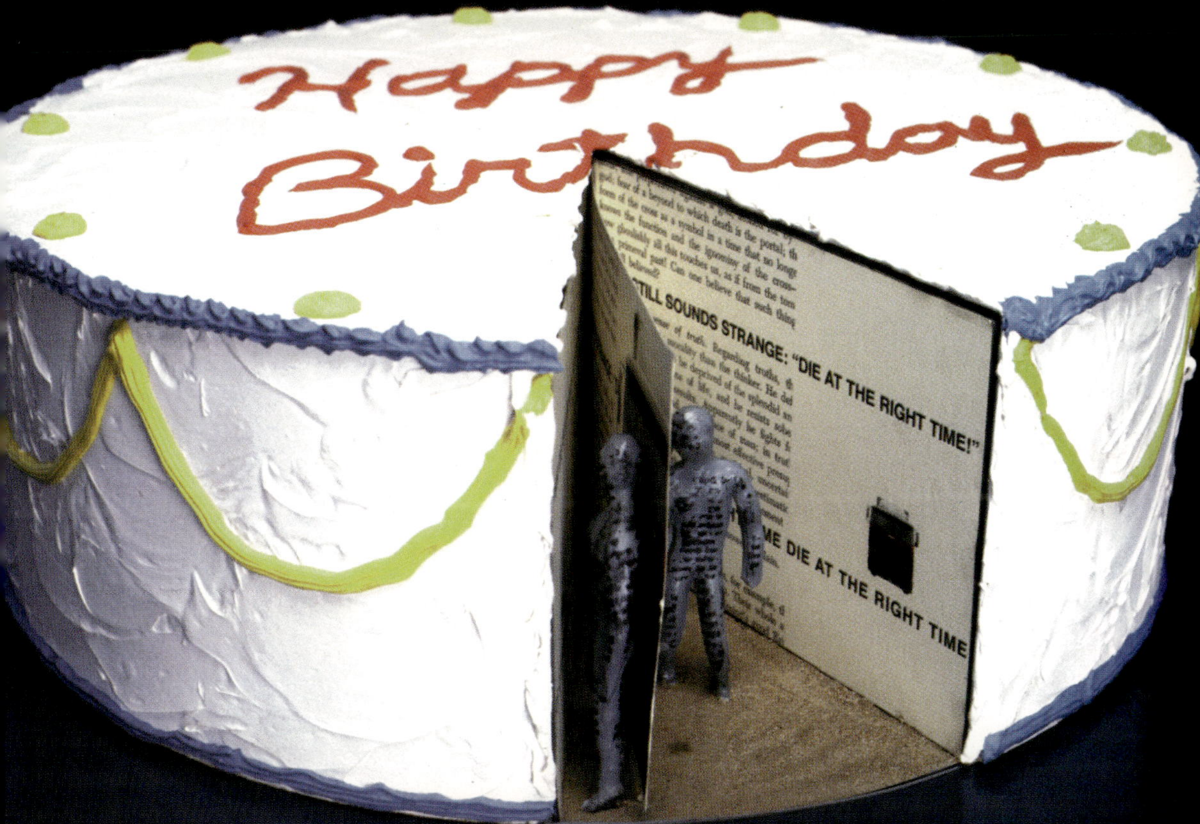

Happy Birthday
...TILL SOUNDS STRANGE: "DIE AT THE RIGHT TIME!"
...DIE AT THE RIGHT TIME

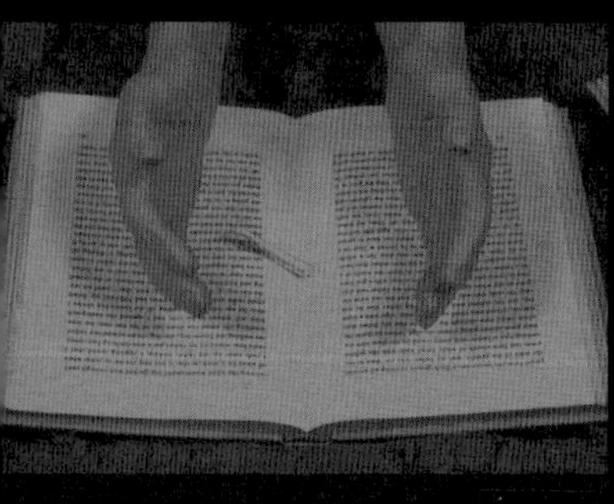

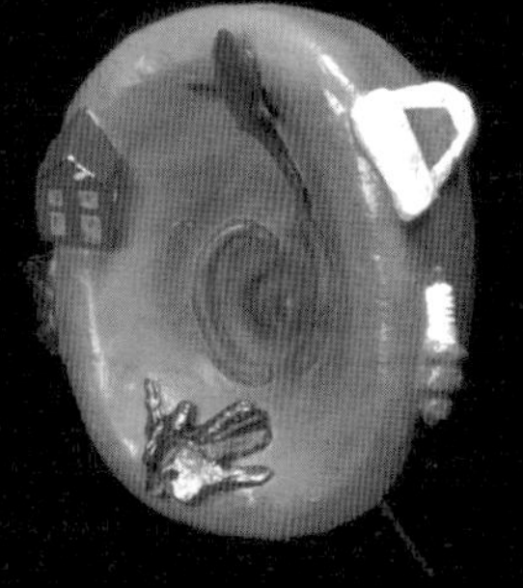

Cake Walk, 1997 *(following two pages)*

own death. A crude figure emerges from the center of a decorated birthday cake with one slice (of life?) removed. The figure dances towards the viewer, only to get mowed down by an approaching truck. The truck appears from the side of the cake and is surrounded by Zarathustra's quotes on voluntary death: "Many die too late and a few die too early. The doctrine still sounds strange: Die at the right time! Of course, how can those who never live at the right time, die at the right time?" It is interesting to note that the title is derived from a nineteenth-century contest among African-Americans in which the most accomplished and creative strut won a cake as the grand prize. In **Cake Walk,** Barsamian dances with fate, mortality, and the responsibility to choose a virtuous direction in one's life.

"My earlier works were very simple and the story lines were approximately one-to one-and-a-half seconds, repeated endlessly. Since then, I have been wrapping the action in a helix around a

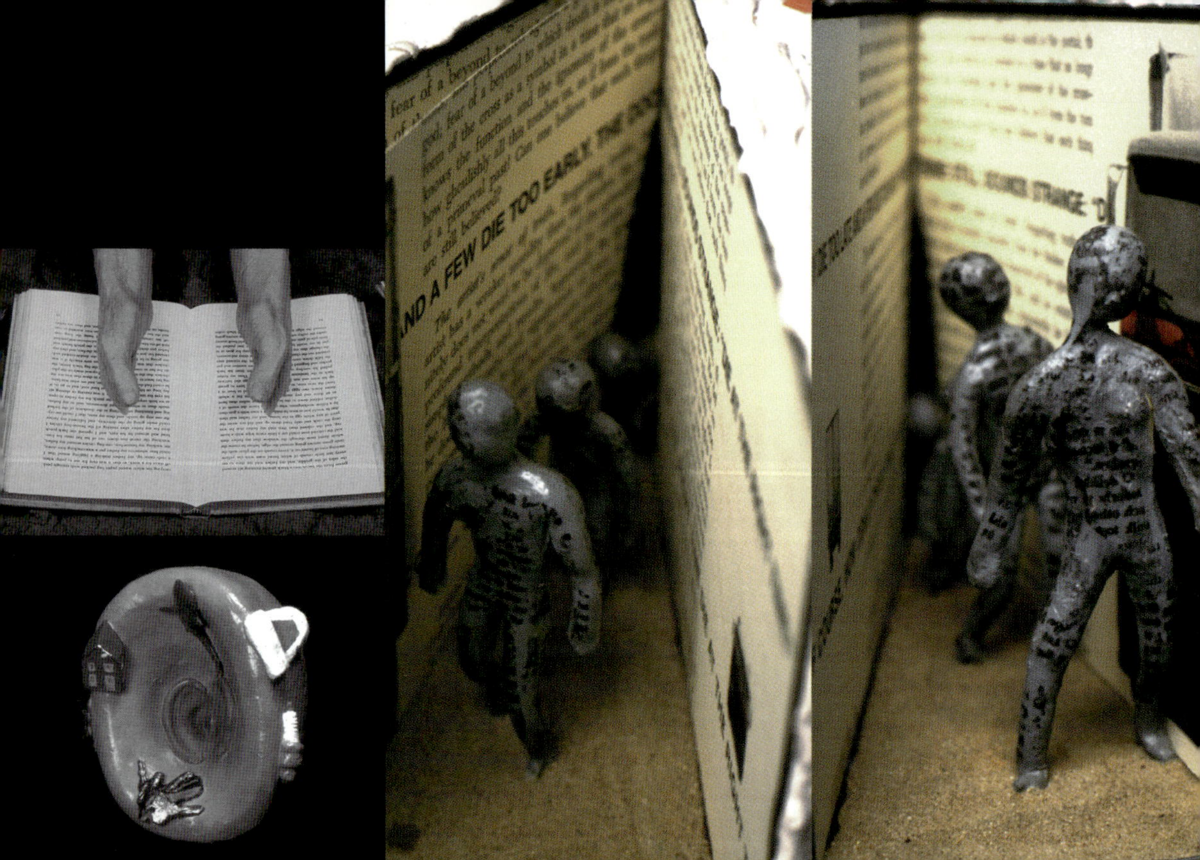
AND A FEW DIE TOO EARLY

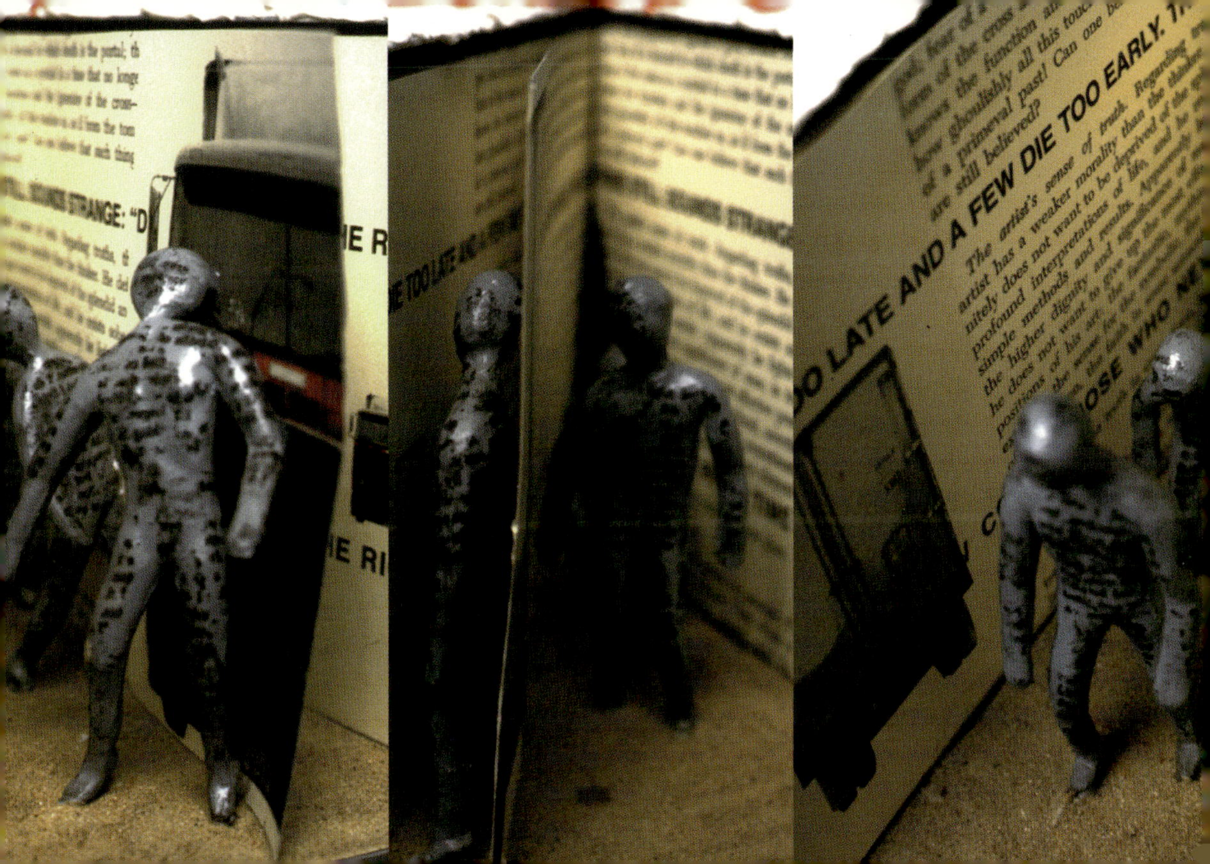
SOUNDS STRANGE: "D
THE RI
E RI
E TOO LATE AND
TOO LATE AND A FEW DIE TOO EARLY. T
The artist's sense of truth
nitely does not want to be deprived of
profound interpretations and results
SOUNDS STRANGE

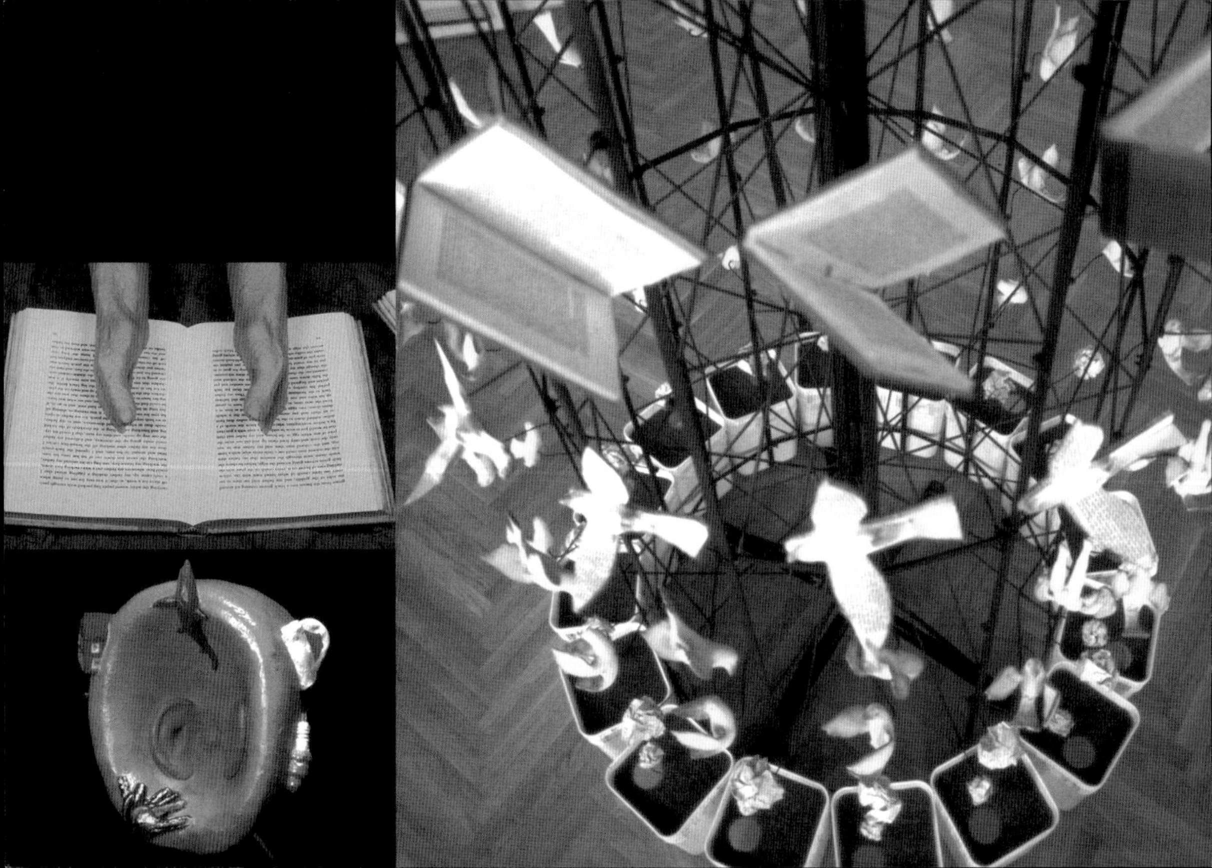

cylinder. As it changes position, it gets several wraps around the cylinder. This extends the visual action by five or six seconds thus creating six to ten seconds of story line to work with."

The discovery of the helix format created greater possibilities for the artist. The action could now be formed vertically, diagonally, and horizontally. Since its initial use in **Transfiguration** (1993), Barsamian has incorporated the helix into most of the ensuing works. In **Two Step** (1997), a photograph of a dancing couple is torn in half. One figure floats downward, shifting as it falls into a fluid that, in turn, fills a glass. The glass overturns, spilling its content. The fluid re-forms into a photograph of the original dancer who joins a new partner. **Two Step** is a sarcastic response to the foibles of immaturity as well as a homage to the wisdom gained though experience. "I was thinking about the ease in which we repeat our behaviors; that the actions that we do, regardless of what we call them, is nature playing itself out," says Barsamian.

Transfiguration (detail), 1993

Two Step (details), 1997 (following two pages)
Collection Raymond Wang, Taipei, Taiwan

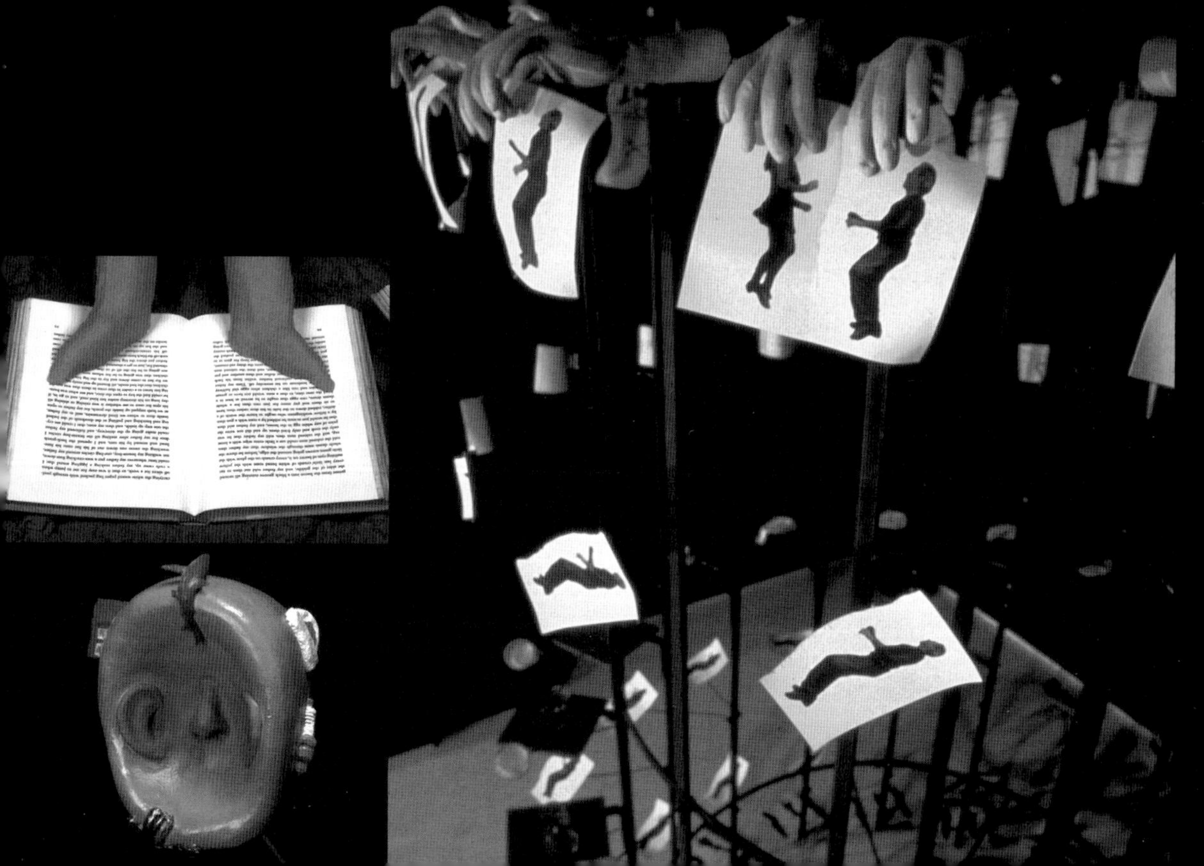

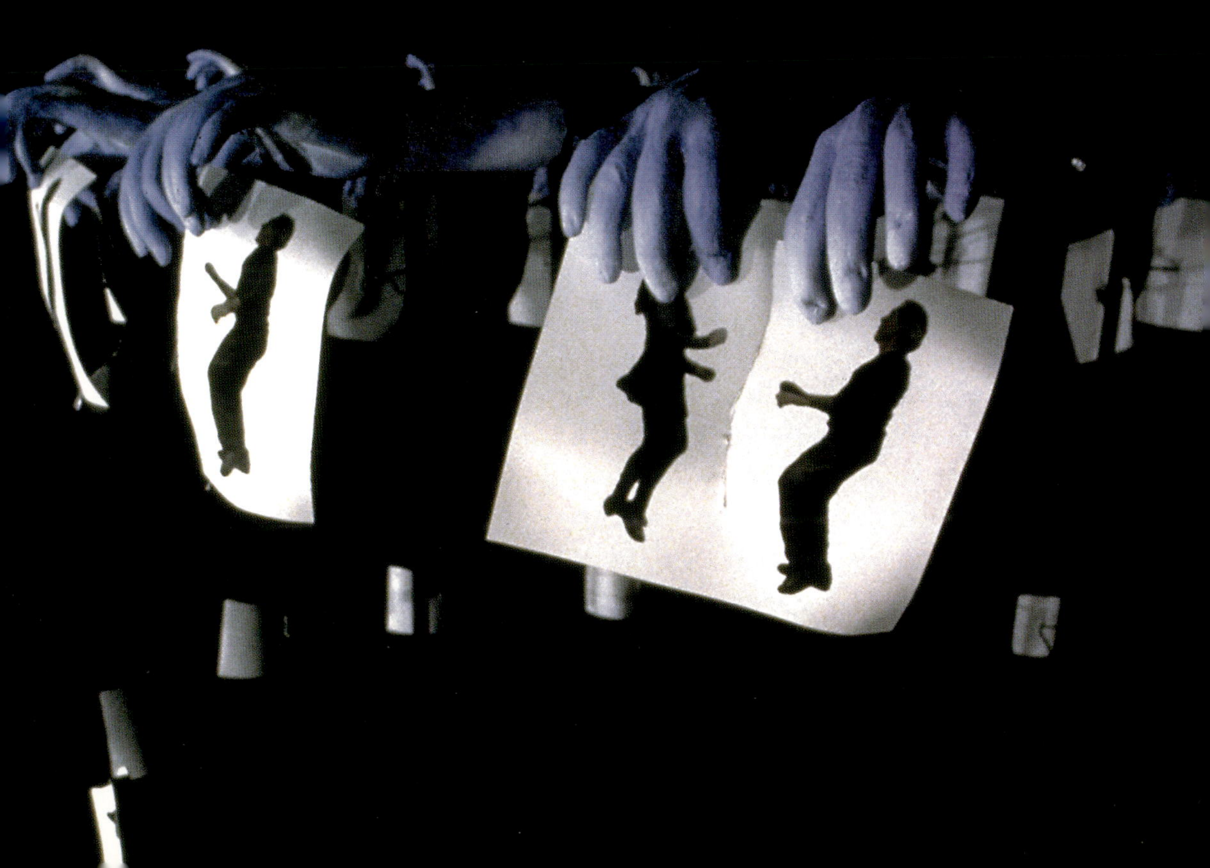

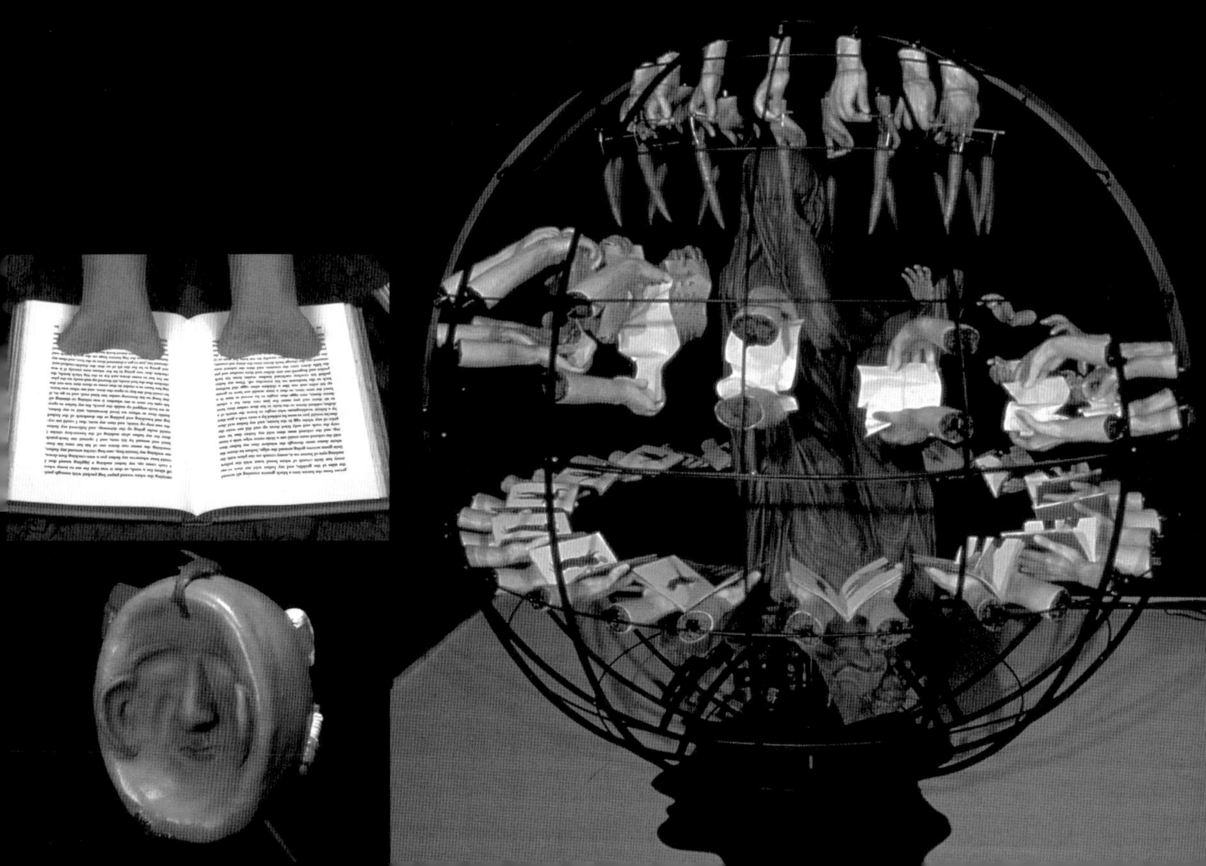

In **No, Never Alone** (1997), the artist places a human form into a spinning cage. The solitary, cloaked figure observes the action occurring all around it. Its face is shrouded, its body unmoving. It is blind. The reference point, however, is not the figure but the animated images that surround it. This action taunts with a dangling carrot, offers an eye chart that can't be read, and ends with an open book. The book sprouts images of hands clapping on one side and a blind dervish on the other.

Hands, used here to encourage the action to continue—to keep the beat, are a reoccurring image in the artist's work. Hands indicate the most expressive and aggressive part of being human. Along with the eyes, they are the most potent symbols of human action.

Die Falle (1998) chronicles a dream within a dream, pitting the pleasures of slumber against the tribulations of our inner activity. The sequence of action begins at the bottom of the work, drifting upward in a helix format. We observe a sleeping head resting on a pillow. From this head emerges a

No, Never Alone, 1997 (left and following two pages)
Courtesy the artist and Schmidt Bingham Gallery

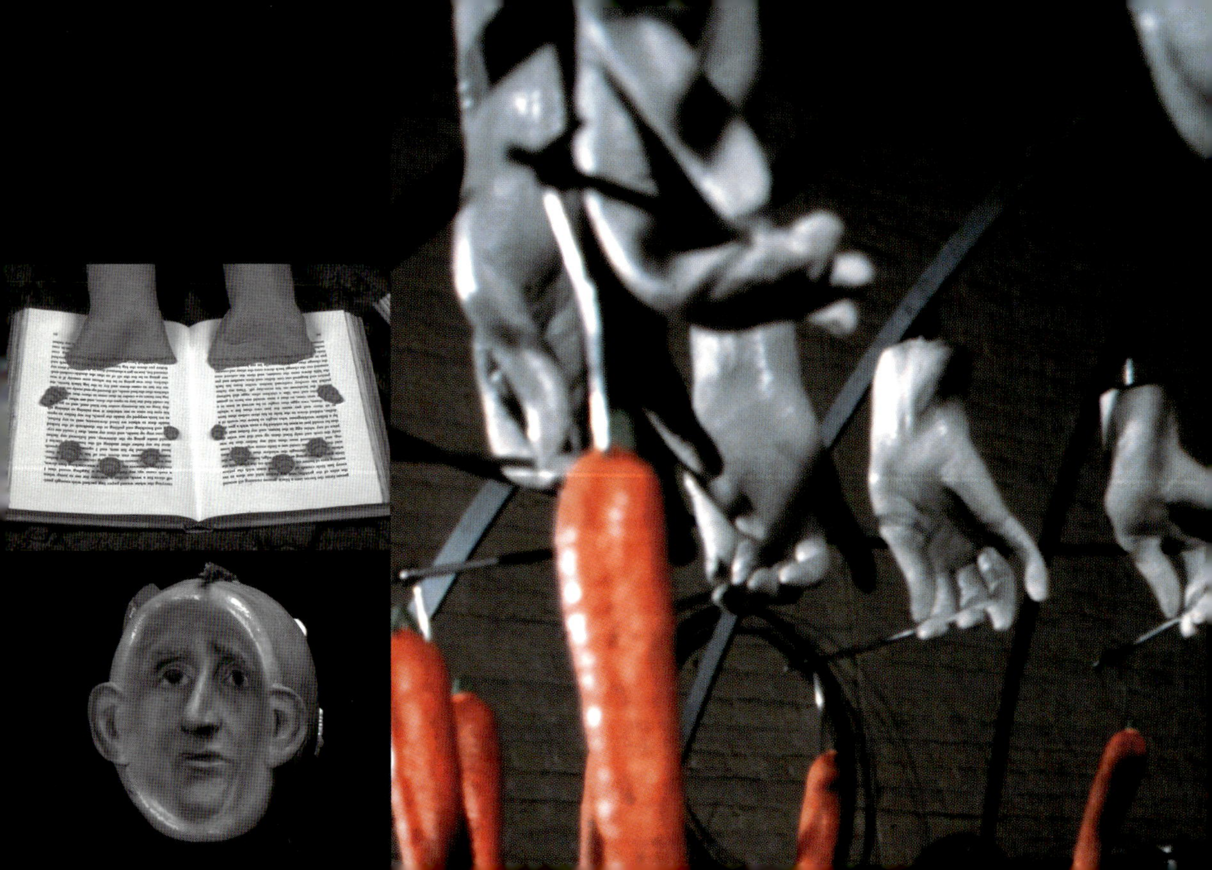

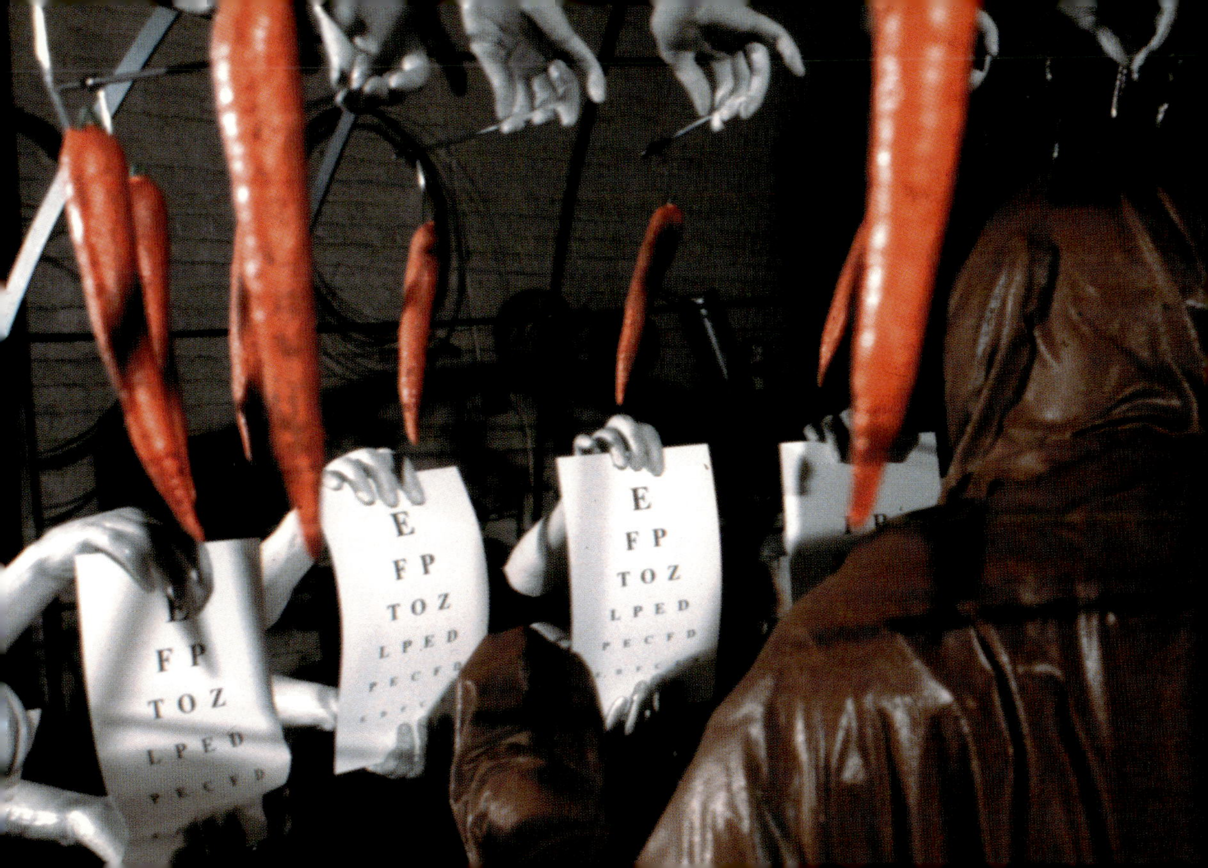
E
F P
T O Z
L P E D
P E C F D
E
F P
T O Z
L P E D
P E C F D
E
F P
T O Z
L P E D
P E C F D

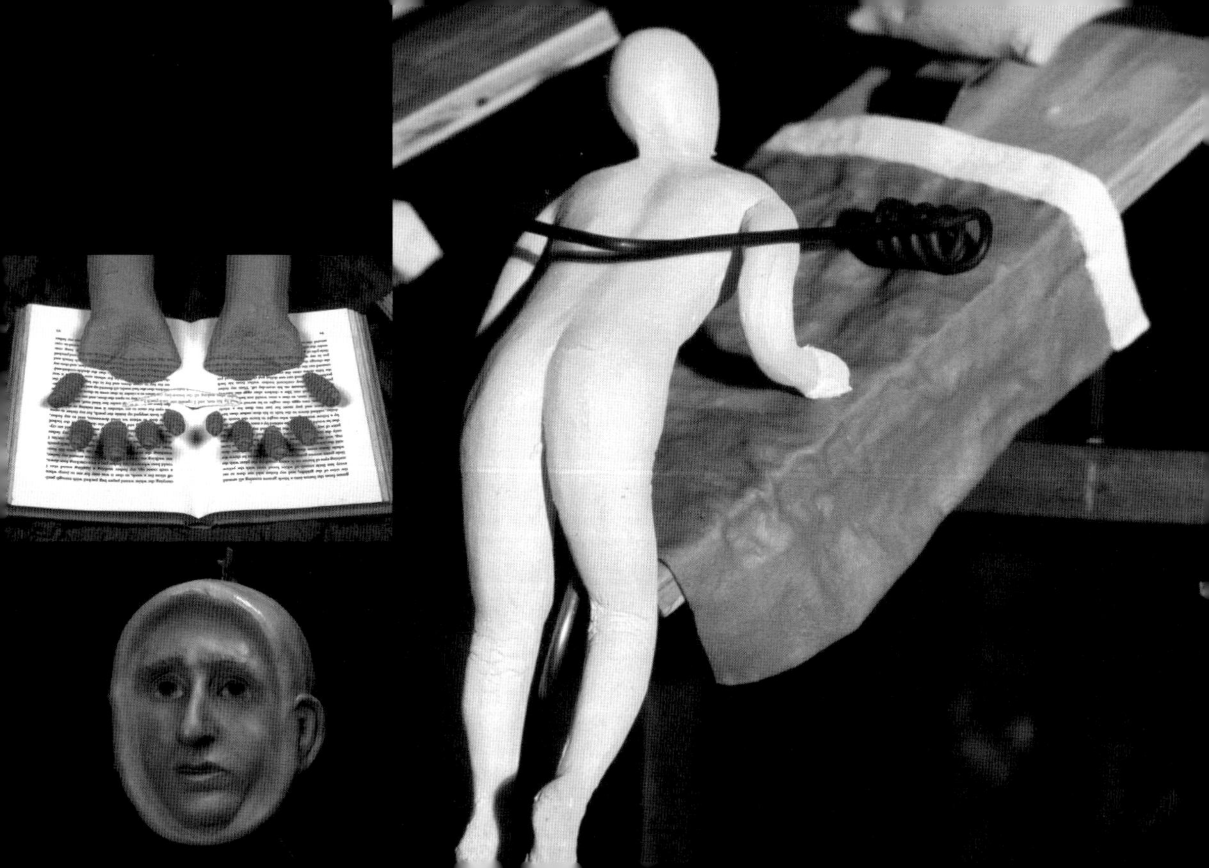

stream of fluid. From the fluid a small figure appears, struggling to free itself from its origin. This figure begins to tuck and roll before becoming a circle, a wheel, and a tire. As the tire begins to roll, it looses its circular shape and becomes squared in appearance. The tire, because of its shape, begins to bump along and "lays rubber" in the form of text. The wheel sequentially metamorphoses back into the original figure that floats toward a combination bed and mousetrap, eventually joining it. (*Die Falle* is German for "the trap," a slang expression for "bed.") With an upward and lofty action, this work suggests that the nocturnal struggle to appease the conflict between the mind and body is inevitable and commonplace.

The Scream (1998) is the second self-portrait produced by the artist. In it, Barsamian literally has too much to say. His open mouth slowly begins to engulf his entire head, playing upon the aphorisms "speaking one's mind" or "baring one's soul." This inside-out, outside-in, turnabout reveals some obstacles: a boot, a half-used tube of toothpaste, a set of keys.

Die Falle (details), 1998 (following two pages)
Courtesy the artist and Schmidt Bingham Gallery

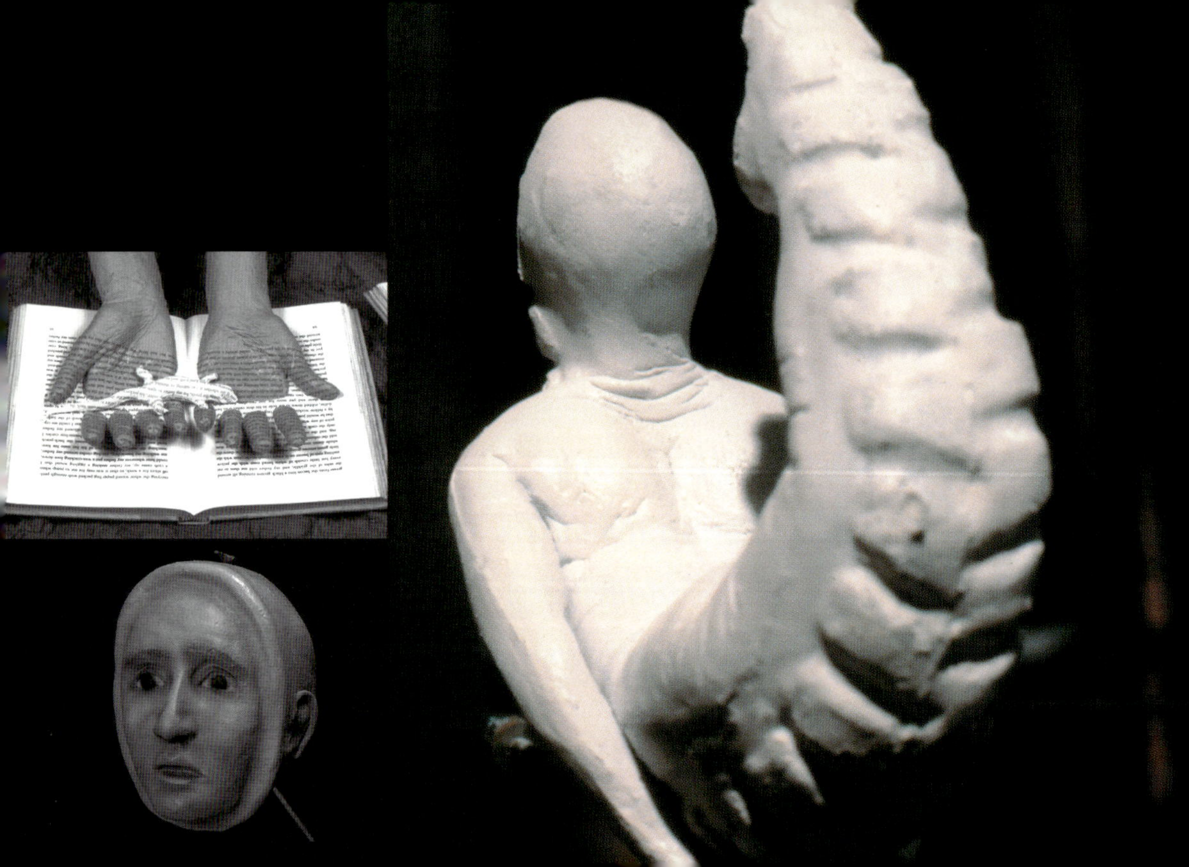

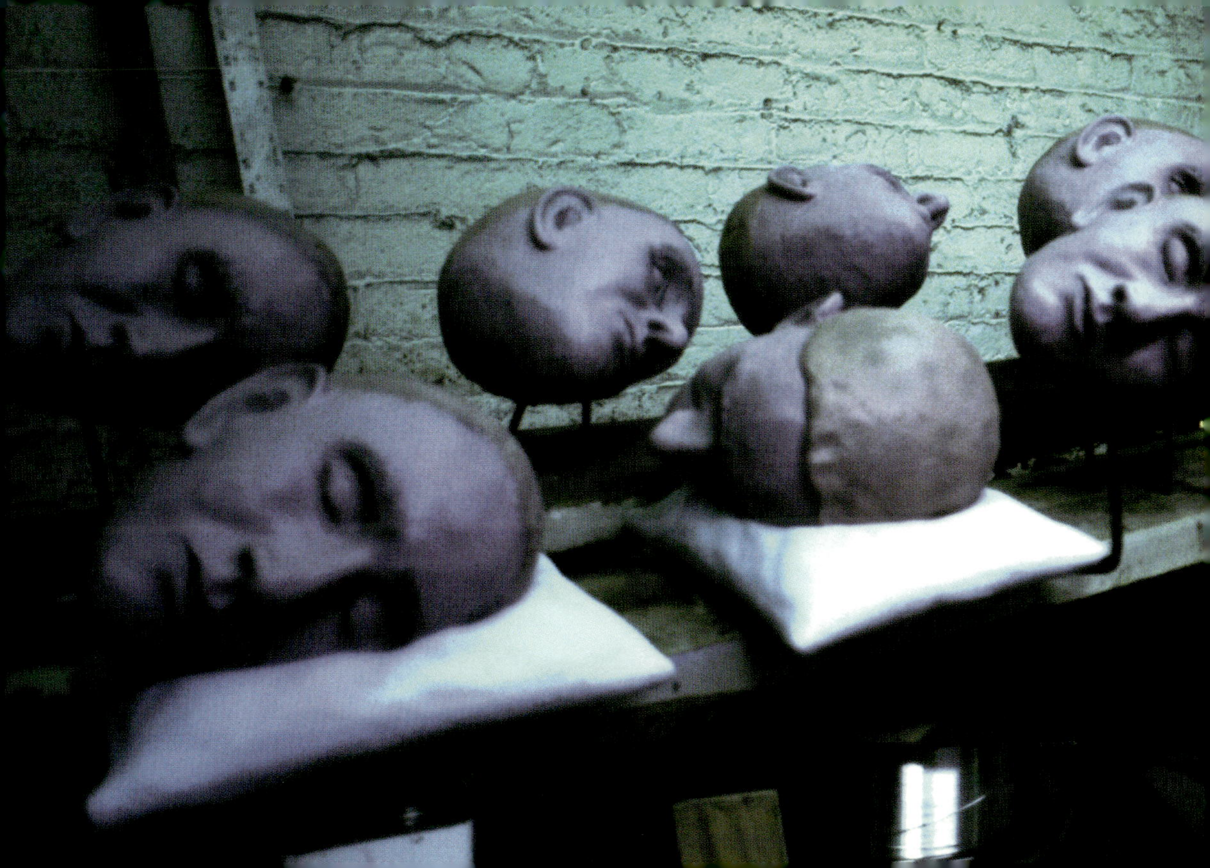

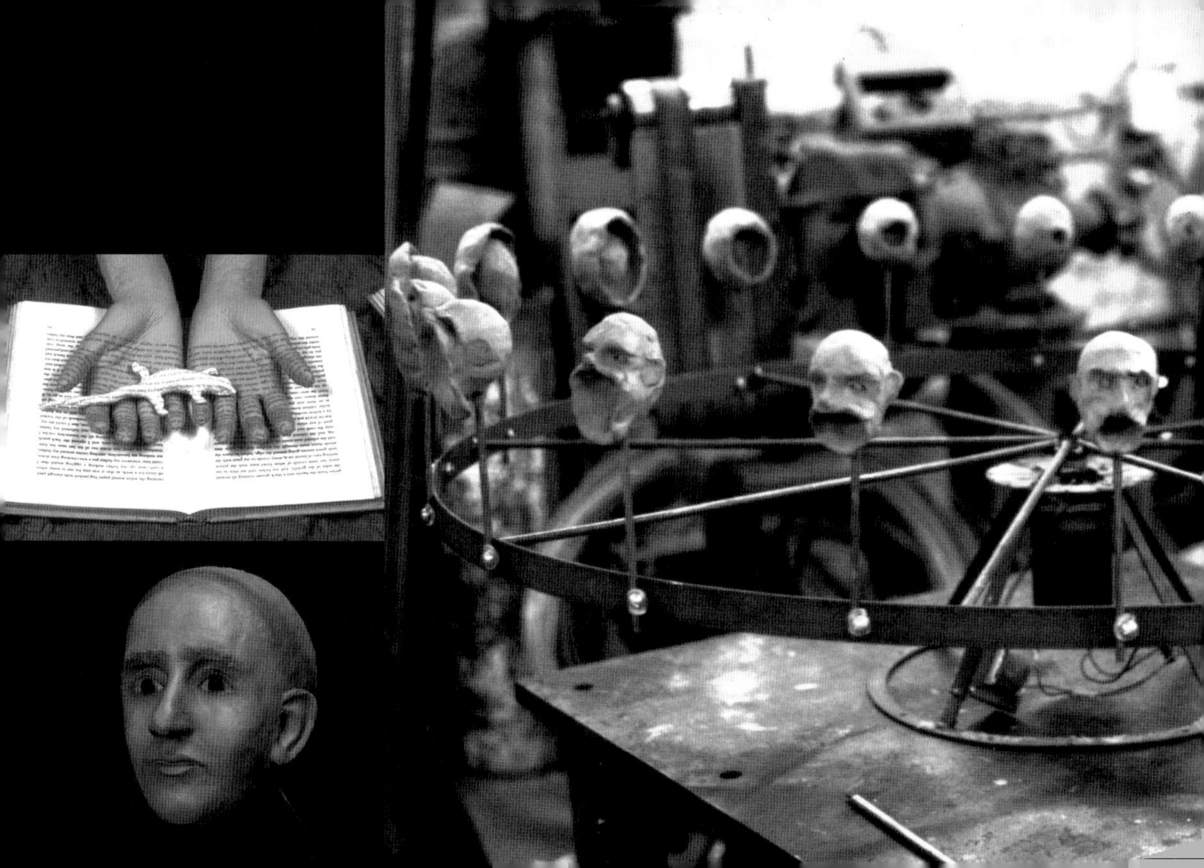

The Scream speaks to the clutter of everyday life, bent on distracting the will from following its more noble pursuits.

The machine in art has many precedents, especially during the past four decades: Think of Jean Tinguely's self-destructive mechanized sculptures, Dennis Oppenheim's electrical deconstruction of pop culture, and Rebecca Horn's poetics. Further back, the Futurists were obsessed with the idea of the machine—seeing it as a hopeful savior from the ills of history. The machines that Barsamian creates have found their own niche and could be described as a visit to a drive-in movie in a souped-up Lincoln loaded with Joseph Cornell's austere surrealist boxes.

Barsamian's images offer us only clues in deciphering his stories. Like the experience of remembering some distant event that changed the course of one's life, the results are just short of comprehension, pregnant with meaning and astonishingly familiar. **Innuendo Non Troppo** echoes a statement once attributed to Tinguely: "The machine allows me, above anything, to reach poetry."

The Scream (work in progress)   *The Scream* (details), 1998 (following two pages)
Courtesy the artist and Schmidt Bingham Gallery

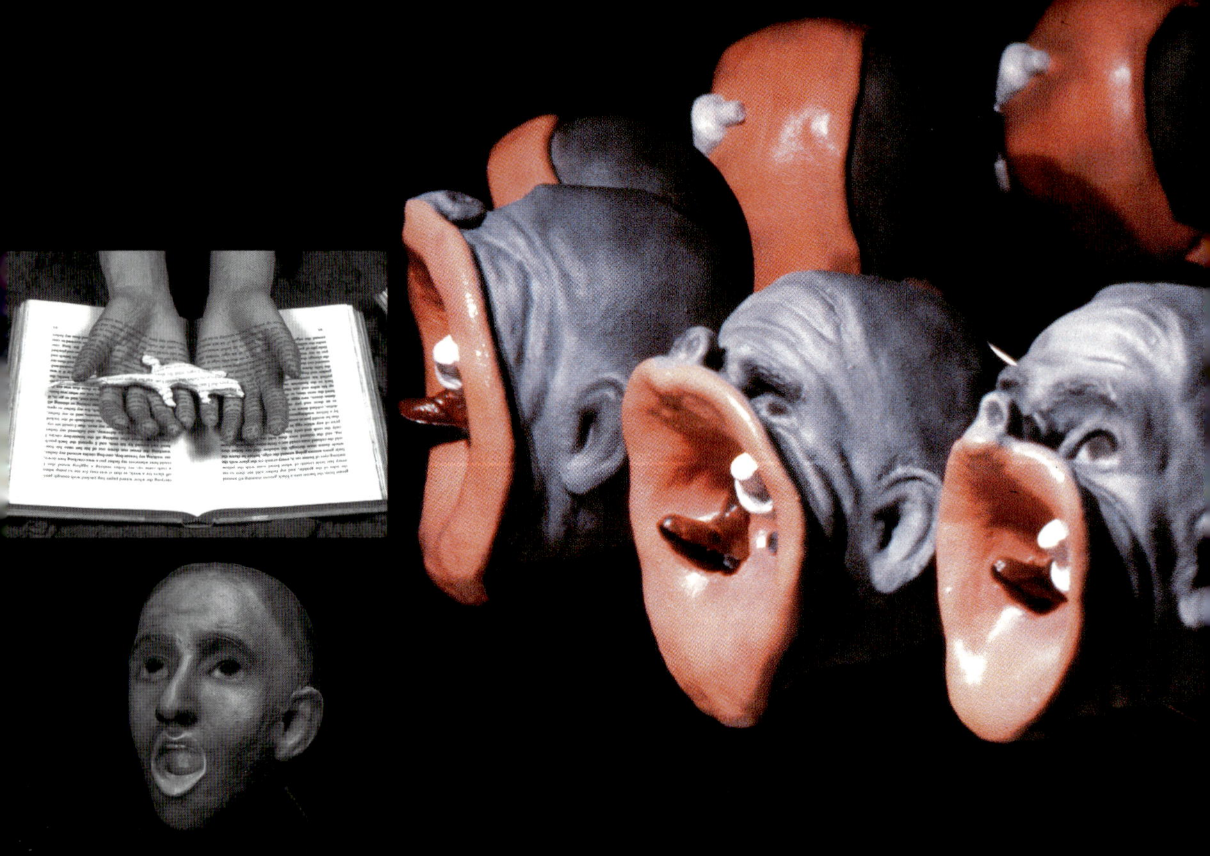

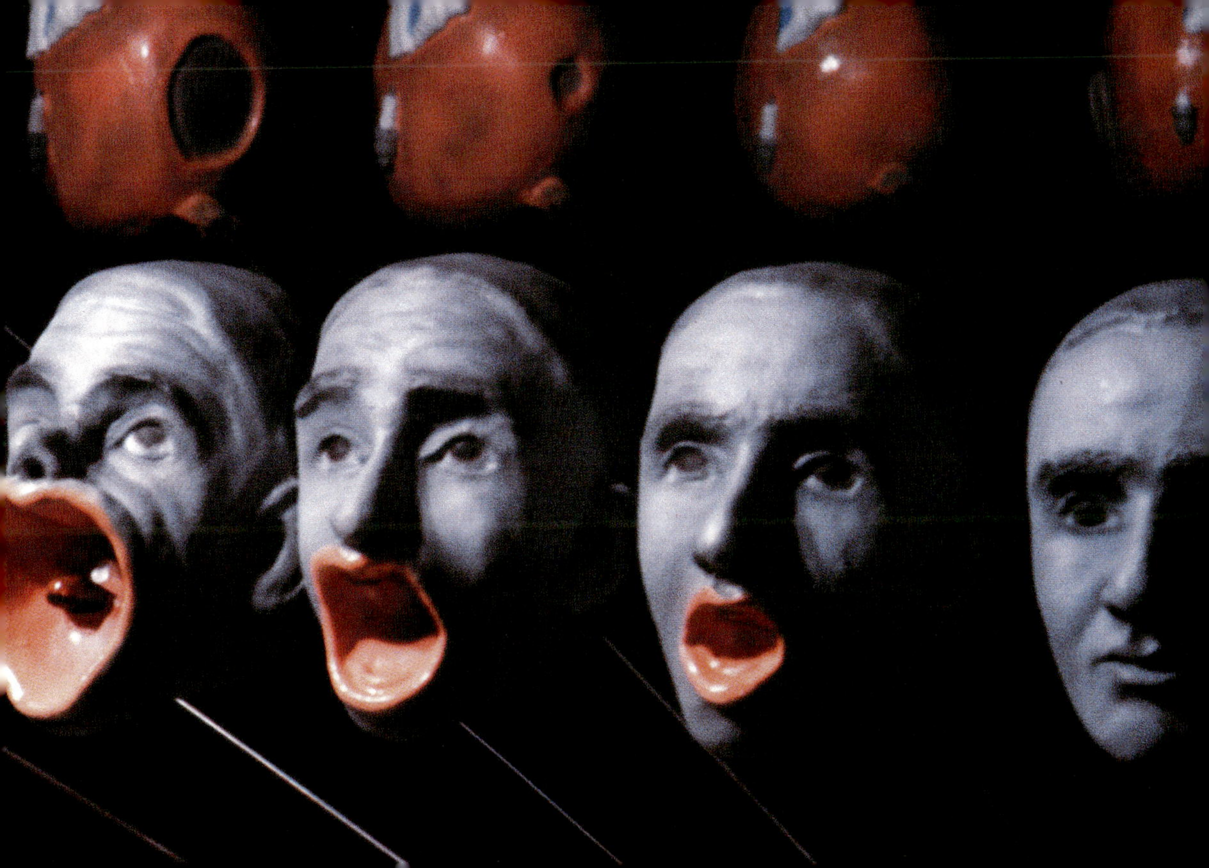

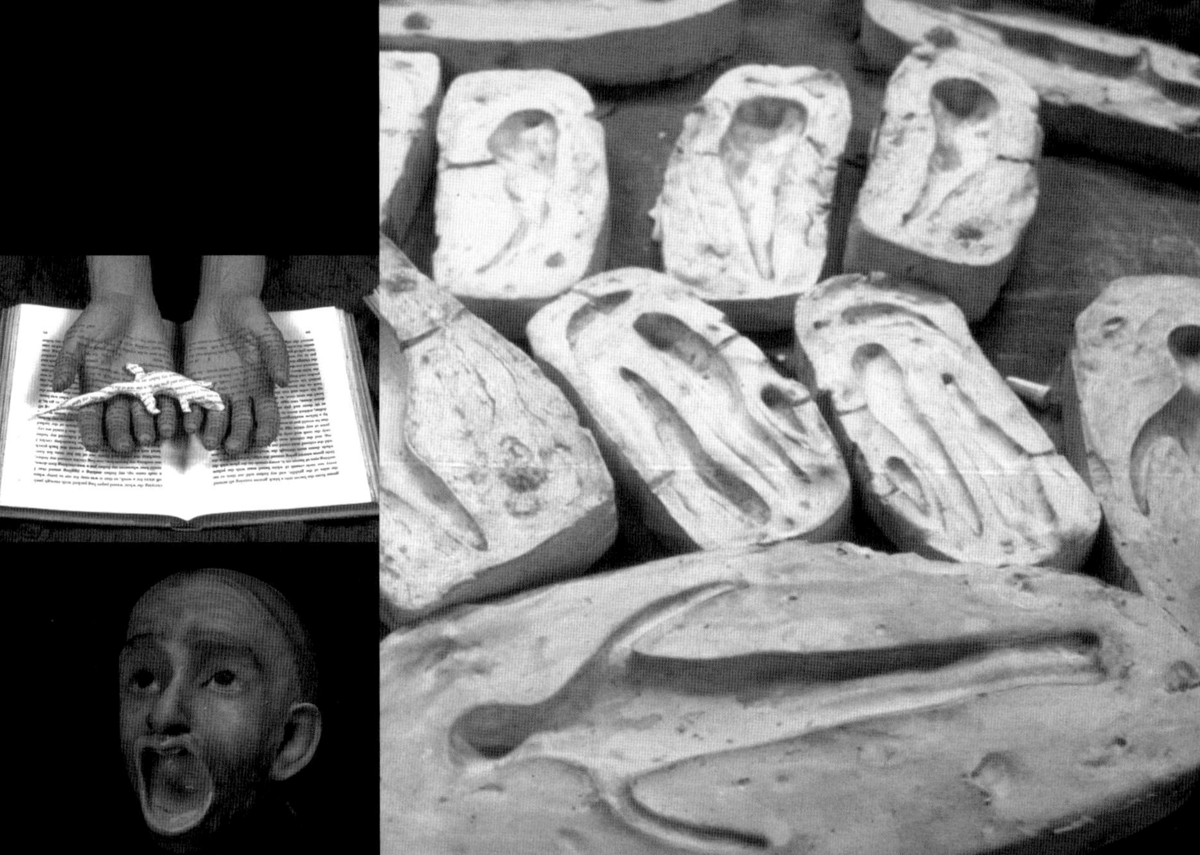

References

Anderson, Laurie. **Stories from the Nerve Bible: A Retrospective, 1972-1992.** New York: HarperPerennial, 1994.

Arnheim, Rudolf. **Art and Visual Perception.** Berkeley and Los Angeles: University of California Press, 1974.

Bender, Gretchen, and Timothy Druckrey, eds. **Culture on the Brink: Ideologies of Technology,** Dia Center for the Arts, Discussions in Contemporary Culture. Seattle: Bay Press, 1994.

Ceram, C.W. **Archaeology of the Cinema.** New York: Harcourt, Brace and World, Inc., 1965.

Crary, Jonathan. **Techniques of the Observer: On Vision and Modernity in the Nineteenth Century,** an October book. Cambridge, MA and London: MIT Press, 1990.

Farber, Janet L. **Gregory Barsamian,** exhibition brochure. Omaha, NE: Joslyn Art Museum, 1997.

Freund, Larry. **Gregory Barsamian,** interview for radio broadcast. Voice of America, 1997.

Hayles, Katherine N. **The Materiality of Informatics.** Baltimore: The Johns Hopkins University Press and the Society for Literature and Science, 1996.

Numerous authors. Friedrich Nietzche, Selected Writings, Bios, Study Guides. World Wide Web public domain sites, 1997-1998.

Reed, Edward S. **James J. Gibson and the Psychology of Perception.** New Haven, CT: Yale University Press, 1988.

Yates, Stephen, ed. **Poetics of Space: A Critical Photographic Anthology.** Albuquerque, NM: University of New Mexico Press, 1995.

Conversations and correspondence between the artist and author, 1991-1998.

Die Falle (work in progress)

Checklist of the Exhibition

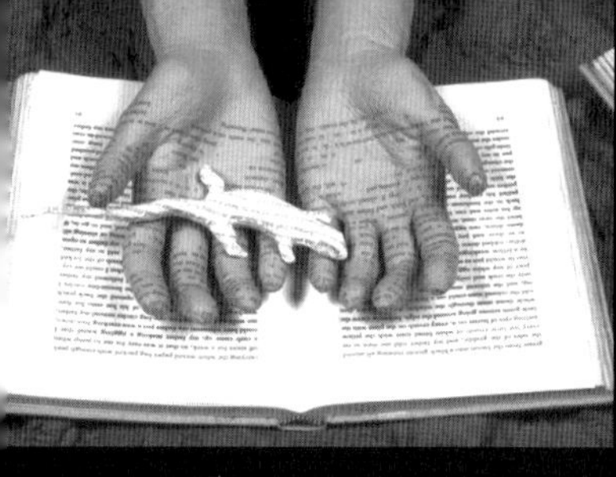

Die Falle (The Trap) 1998
fabric, acrylic, urethane foam, steel, motor,
strobe light, with soundtrack by Bruce Darby
104 x 80 inches diameter
Courtesy the artist and Schmidt Bingham Gallery, NY

Orphan 1998
paper, acrylic, urethane foam, steel, motor,
strobe light
60 x 120 inches diameter
Courtesy the artist and Schmidt Bingham Gallery, NY

The Scream 1998
acrylic, urethane foam, steel, motor, strobe light,
with soundtrack by Bruce Darby
64 x 126 inches diameter
Courtesy the artist and Schmidt Bingham Gallery, NY

Cake Walk 1997
urethane foam, wood, paper, acrylic, steel, motor,
strobe light
45 x 26 inches diameter
Collection of Howard and Judy Tullman, Chicago, IL

No, Never Alone 1997
paper, acrylic, urethane foam, steel, motor, strobe light
84 x 80 inches diameter
Courtesy the artist and Schmidt Bingham Gallery, NY

Two Step 1997
paper, acrylic, urethane foam, aluminum, steel,
motor, strobe light, with soundtrack by Bruce Darby
102 x 84 inches diameter
Collection Raymond Wang, Taipei, Taiwan

Coprophagia 1991
photographs, acrylic, polymer resin, newspaper,
wood, aluminum, motor, strobe light
63 x 74 inches diameter
Courtesy the artist and Schmidt Bingham Gallery, NY

Dipping Digits (Always Gets Wet) 1991
paper, acrylic, urethane foam, steel, motor, strobe light
48 x 84 inches diameter
Courtesy the artist and Schmidt Bingham Gallery, NY

Putti 1991
acrylic, urethane foam, steel cable, motor, strobe light
72 x 216 inches diameter
Courtesy the artist and Schmidt Bingham Gallery, NY

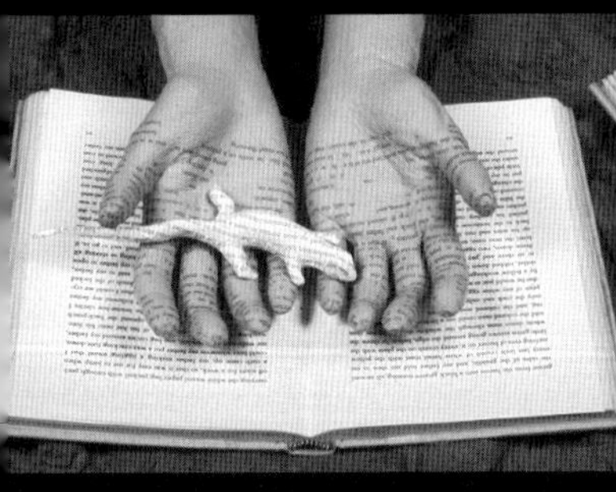

In bringing this show together I would like to offer my deepest thanks to the following: My friends Mary Ziegler, Robin Perl, Bob Beswick, Marechal Brown, Doris Villa, Nancy Barsamian, and Perry Hoberman, as well as my assistants Russell Barbara, Chris Brophy, and Pablo Ramella. I'd also like to thank composer Bruce Darby for his collaboration on **Die Falle, The Scream,** and **Two Step**.

–Gregory Barsamian

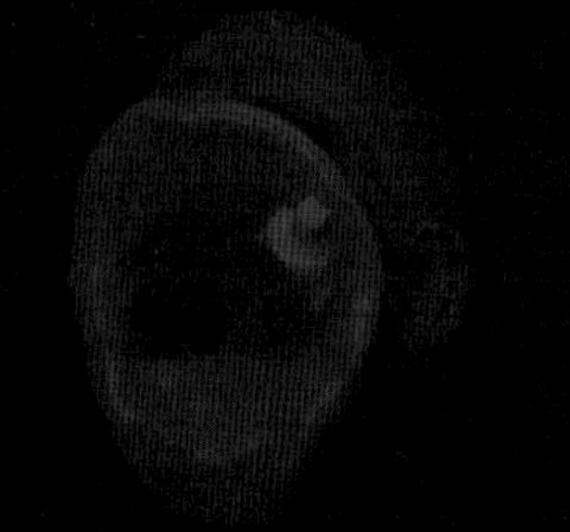

No, Never Alone (*work in progress*)

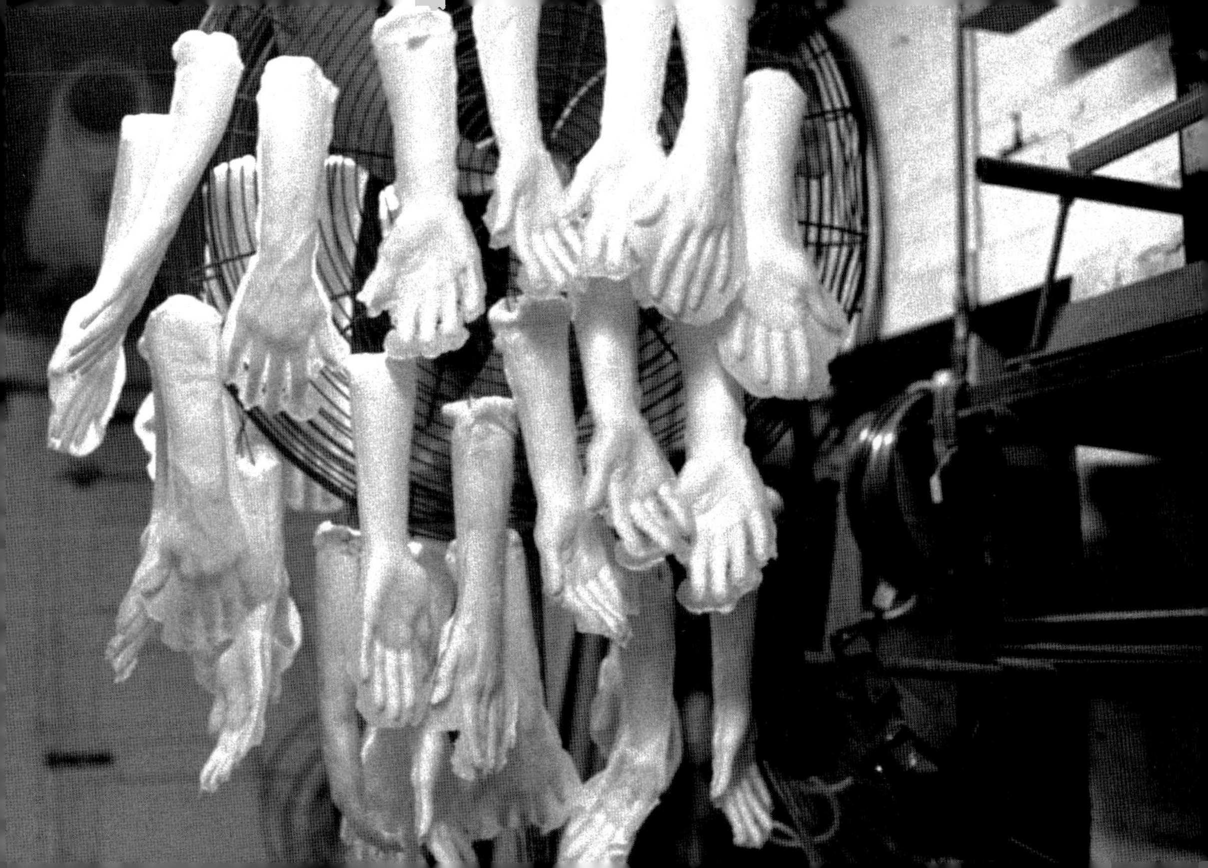

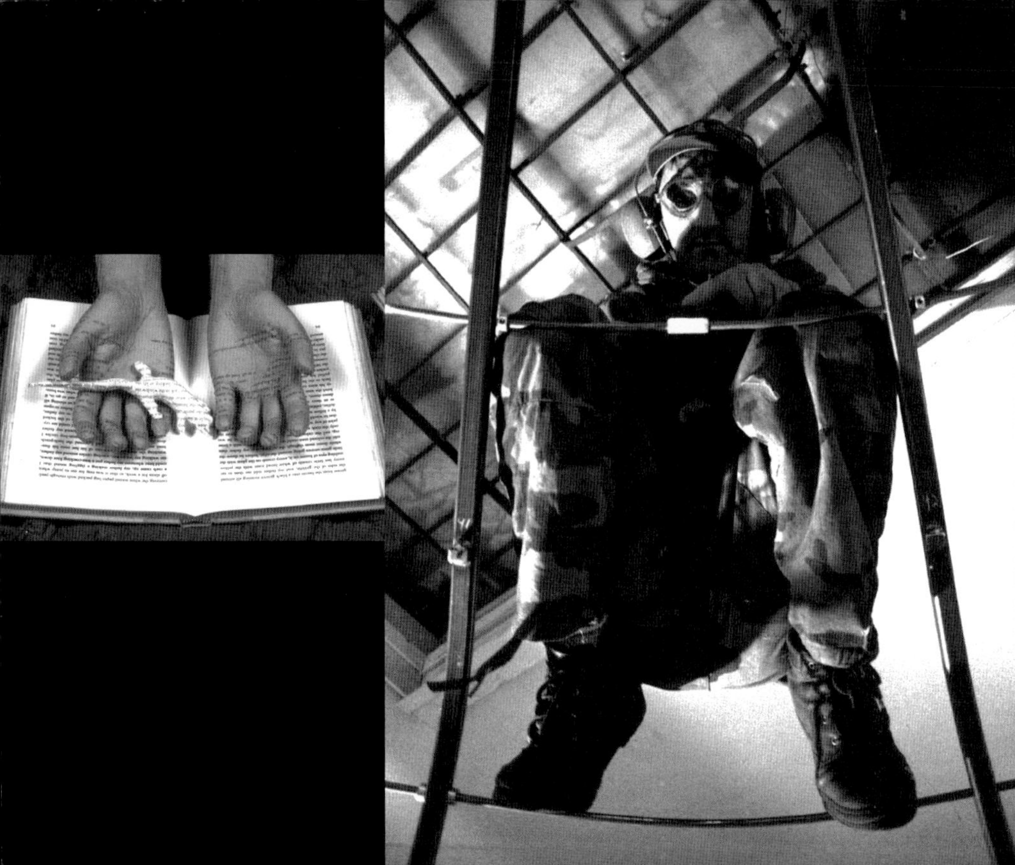

Gregory Barsamian

Born: 1953, Chicago, Illinois

Education: BA in Philosophy, University of Wisconsin-Madison, 1979

Currently resides in Brooklyn, New York

Selected Solo Exhibitions

1998-2000　**Innuendo Non Troppo: The Work of Gregory Barsamian,** The
　　　　　Contemporary Arts Center, Cincinnati, OH (catalogue; traveling to
　　　　　The Arkansas Art Center, Little Rock, AR; Polk Museum of Art,
　　　　　Lakeland, FL; Anderson Gallery, Virginia Commonwealth
　　　　　University, Richmond, VA; Boise Art Museum, Boise, ID; San Jose
　　　　　Museum of Art, San Jose, CA)

1997　　　Schmidt Bingham Gallery, New York, NY

　　　　　20/21: Gregory Barsamian, Joslyn Art Museum, Omaha, NE

1994　　　**Transfigurations,** Cohen Gallery, New York, NY

1992　　　**Persistence of Vision,** Nelson Arts Center, Arizona State University,
　　　　　Tempe, AZ

1991　　　**Behind the Iris,** Bess Cutler Gallery, New York, NY

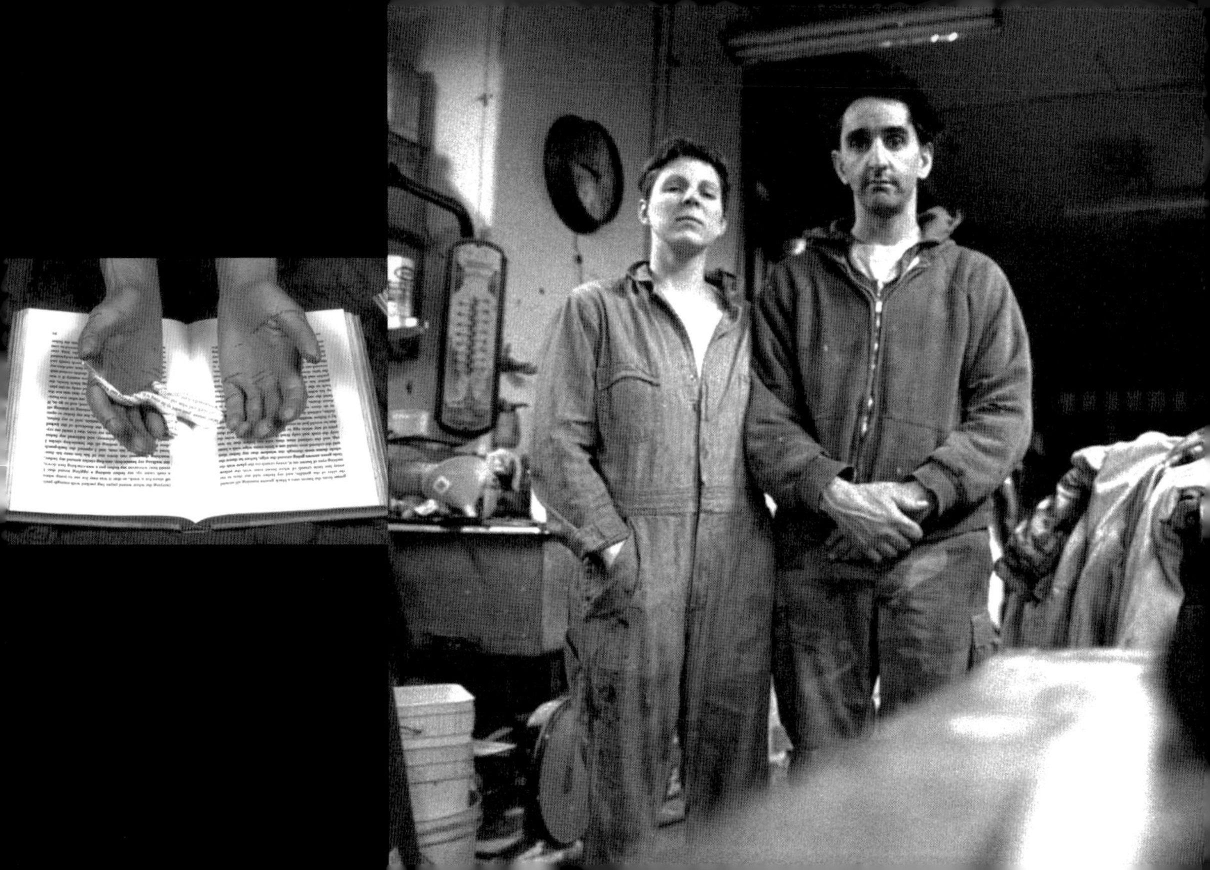

Selected Group Exhibitions

1998   **Festival International Exit** 1998, Maison des Arts, Creteil, France;
Mauberge, France

1997   **Artists Respond to 2001: A Space Odyssey,** Williamsburg Art and
Historical Society, Brooklyn, NY

Wit, Whimsy and Humor, Castle Gallery, College of New Rochelle,
New Rochelle, NY

1996   **Peep Show,** Schmidt Bingham Gallery, New York, NY

Light & Sound, Susquehanna Art Museum, Harrisburg, PA

Image du Future, La Cité des Arts et des Nouvelles Technologies de
Montréal, Montréal, Québec, Canada

Behind the Screen, American Museum of the Moving Image,
Astoria, NY (long-term exhibition)

1995   **Cinimagie,** Musée Chateau, Annecy, France

Forces, Humphrey Gallery, New York, NY/Reading, PA

Art and Technology, Staller Center for the Arts, Stony Brook, NY

Sculpture on the Move, Hudson River Museum, Hudson River
Museum, Yonkers, NY

Gregory Barsamian with sculptor Mary Ziegler in the artist's studio.

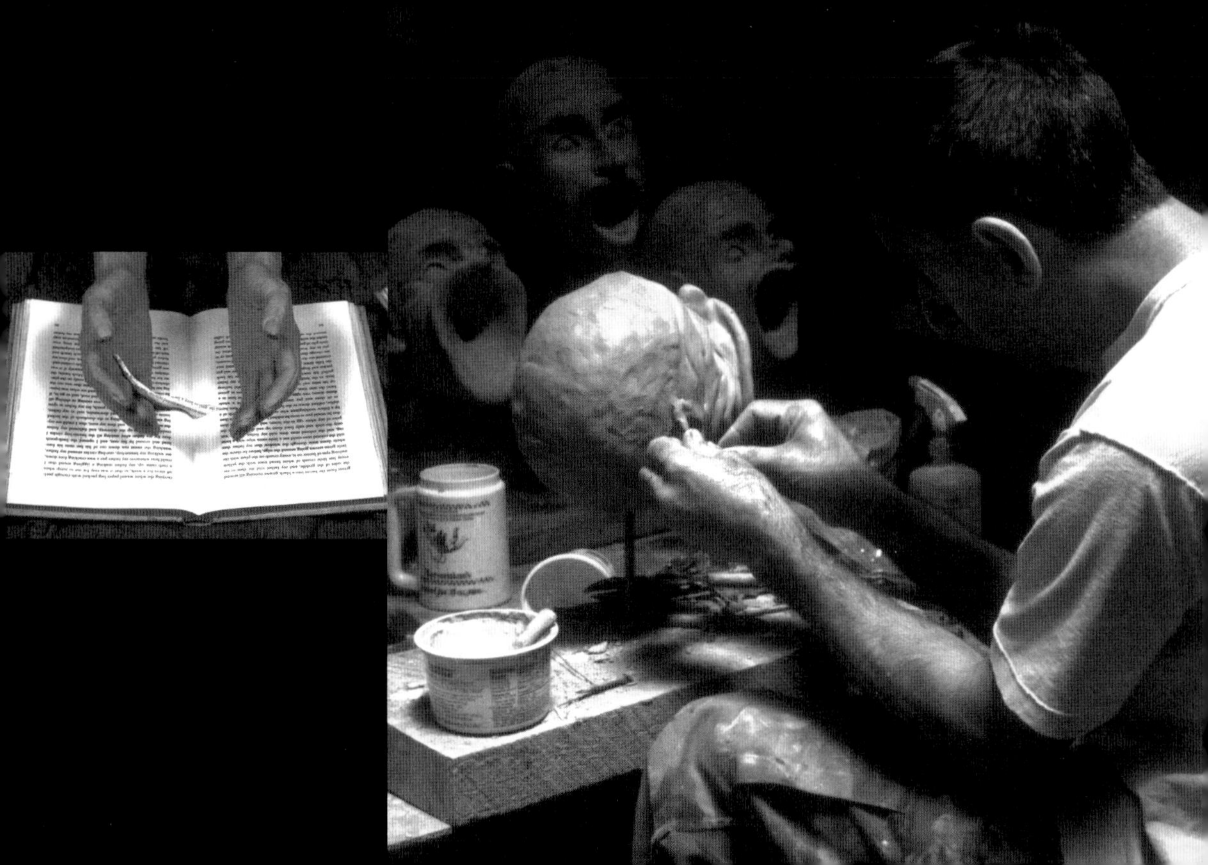

| 1994 | **Circular Logic: Revolutionary Motion in a Linear World,** University of Connecticut, Storrs, CT |

1994   **Circular Logic: Revolutionary Motion in a Linear World,** University of Connecticut, Storrs, CT

1993   **In Out of the Cold,** Center for the Arts, Yerba Buena Gardens, San Francisco, CA

Image du Future, La Cité des Arts et des Nouvelle Technologies de Montréal, Montréal, Québec, Canada

Montage 93, Visual Studies Workshop, Rochester, NY

The Illusionists, John Michael Kohler Arts Center, Sheboygan, WI

Springworks 93, New York Hall of Science, Flushing Meadows Corona Park, NY

1992   **Music-Art Convergence,** Germans van Eck Gallery, NY

Beyond Glory: Re-Presenting Terrorism, Maryland Institute, College of Art, Baltimore, MD

1991   **Mechanika,** The Contemporary Arts Center, Cincinnati, OH

Tweaking the Human, Minor Injury Gallery, Brooklyn, NY

The New Eccentricity: Sculpture, Bess Cutler Gallery, New York, NY

1989   Bess Cutler Gallery, New York, NY

The Scream (work in progress)

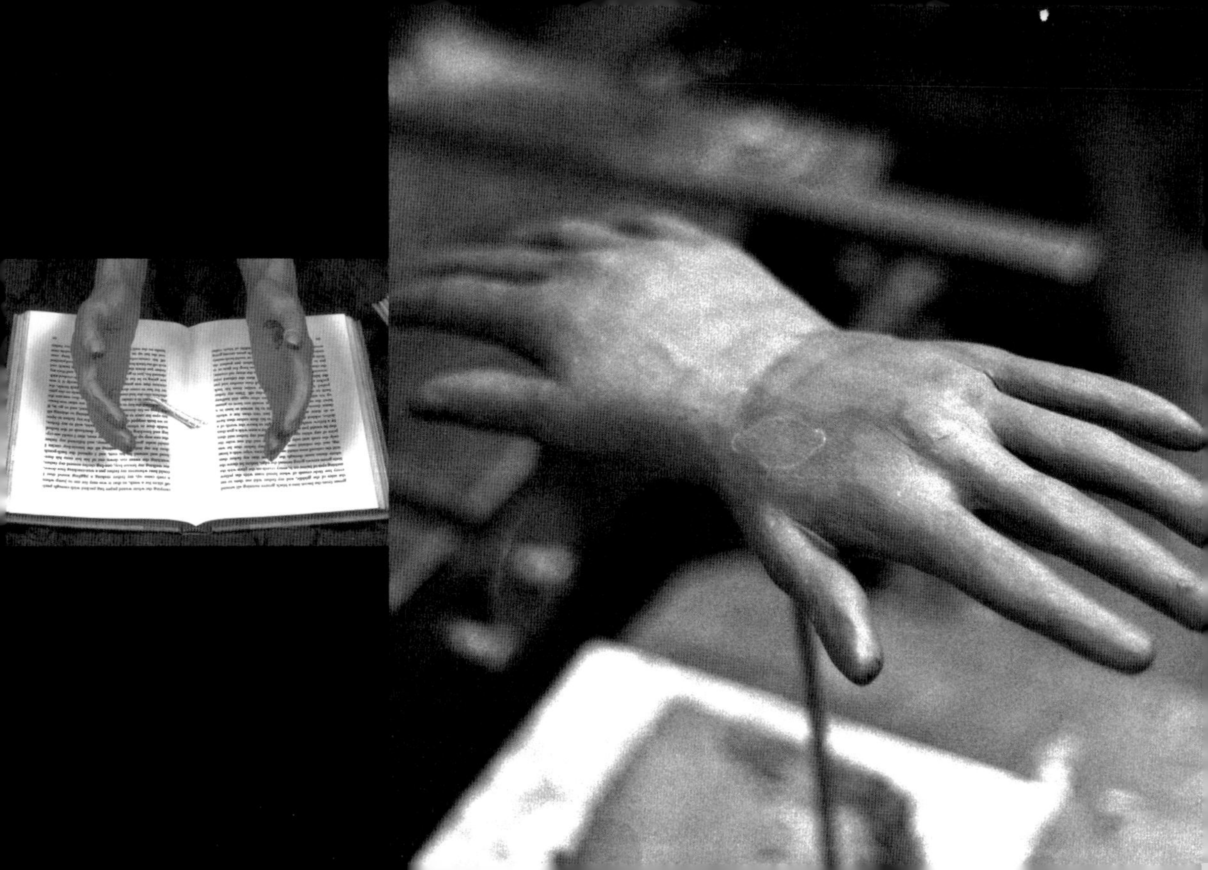

Selected Bibliography

Apgar, Garry, Shaun O'L. Higgins, and Colleen Striegel. **The Newspaper in Art.**
Spokane, WA: New Media Ventures, Inc., 1997.

Auer, James. Exhibition review. **The Milwaukee Journal,** 11 July 1993.

Baker, Kenneth. *Critic's Preview.* **San Francisco Chronicle**, 12 October 1993.

Berkson, Bill. *The Salon at Mission and Third.* **Art in America** 82, no. 6 (June 1994): 40-43.

Blankstein, Amy. *Commissions.* **Sculpture** 16, no. 6 (July/August 1997): 16.

Blumenthal, Ralph. *Anyone Can Become a Star in Astoria.* **The New York Times**,
19 April 1996.

Boardman, Andrew. *Gregory Barsamian.* **New Observations: Popular Metaphysics**, Summer
1997.

Bonetti, David. *A Daring Leap 'In Out of the Cold.'* San Francisco Examiner, 12 October 1993.

Braff, Phyllis. *Casting a Spell: From Lasers and Video to Light and Shadows.* **The New York
Times**, 22 October 1995.

Brenson, Michael. *Greg Barsamian.* **The New York Times**, 15 March 1991.

Delean, Paul. Exhibition preview. **The Montréal Gazette**, 11 May 1993.

Felleman, Susan, and Peter Chametsky. *Szene Brooklyn.* **ZYMA,** November/December 1991.

Farina, Robert. *The Illusionists.* **The Sheboygan Press,** 18 July 1993.

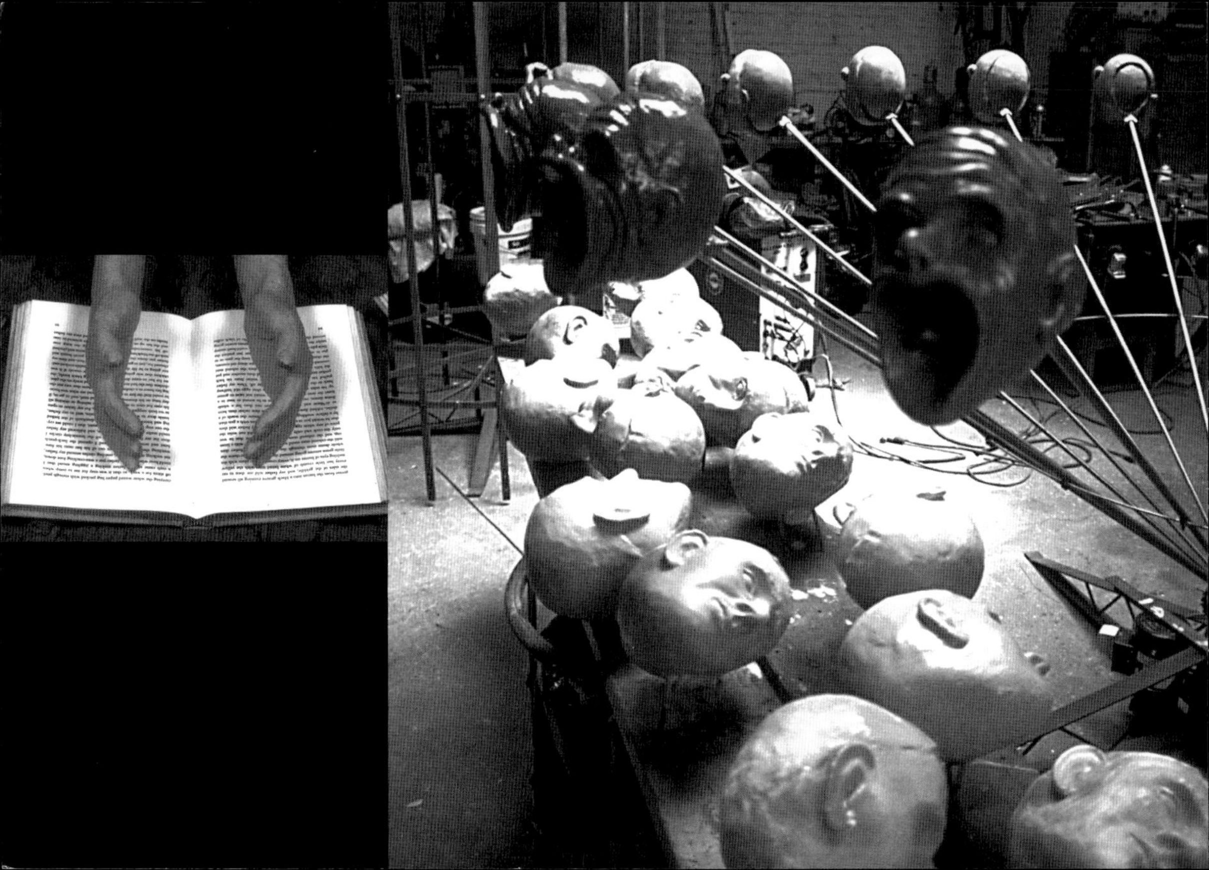

ICC Concept Book: Exploring the Future of the Imagination. Exhibition catalogue. Tokyo, Japan: Nippon Telegraph and Telephone InterCommunication Center, 1997.

James, Jamie. *Goings on About Town: Peep Show.* **The New Yorker,** 29 July 1996.

Levin, Kim. *Choices.* **The Village Voice,** 26 March 1991.

———. *Choices.* **The Village Voice,** 1 March 1994.

MacAdam, Barbara A. Exhibition review. **ARTnews** 93, no. 9 (November 1994): 160

Mahoney, Robert. Exhibition review. **Arts Magazine** 65, no. 10 (Summer 1991): 87

McWilliams, Martha. *Terror to Scale.* **New Art Examiner** 19, no. 4 (April 1992): 14-17

Nilsen, Richard. *Gallery Briefs.* **The Arizona Republic,** 8 November 1992.

Pyne, Lynn. Exhibition review. **The Phoenix Gazette,** 12 November 1992.

Rivlin, Michael. *A Moving Experience.* **Art & Antiques** 20, no. 7 (Summer 1997): 90-95.

Shapiro, Michele. *Astoria's Secret.* **Time Out New York** (17-24 April 1996): 15.

Shimon, J., and L. Linderman. Exhibition review. **New Art Examiner** 21, no. 4 (December 1993): 37.

Sozanski, Edward. Exhibition review. **The Philadelphia Inquirer,** 18 August 1995.

Taylor, Simon. *Review of Exhibitions: Gregory Barsamian.* **Art in America** 79, no. 12 (December 1991): 113-114.

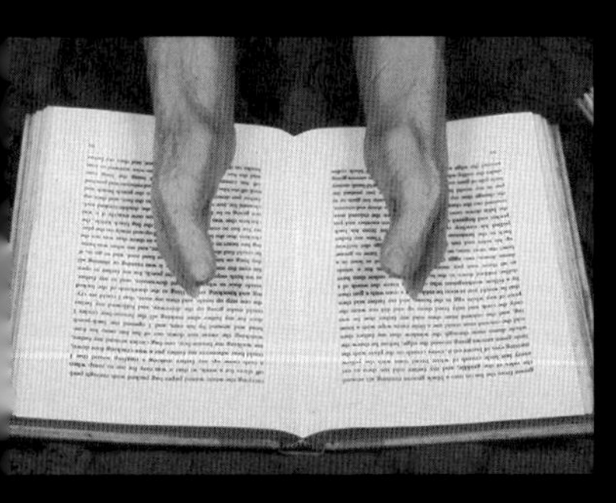

Staff

Charles Desmarais, Director
Jeffrey Arnett, Store Manager
Bettina Bellucci, Development Assistant
David J. Brown, Curator
Lisa Buck, Curator of Education
Kim Humphries, Exhibitions Designer
Kellye Johnson, Assistant to the Director
Michelle Padilla, Publicity Assistant
Julia S. Ranz, Assistant Curator of Education
Natalie L. Schwab, Capital Campaign Director
Jean Spohr, Accountant
Leah Stoddard, Assistant Curator and Registrar

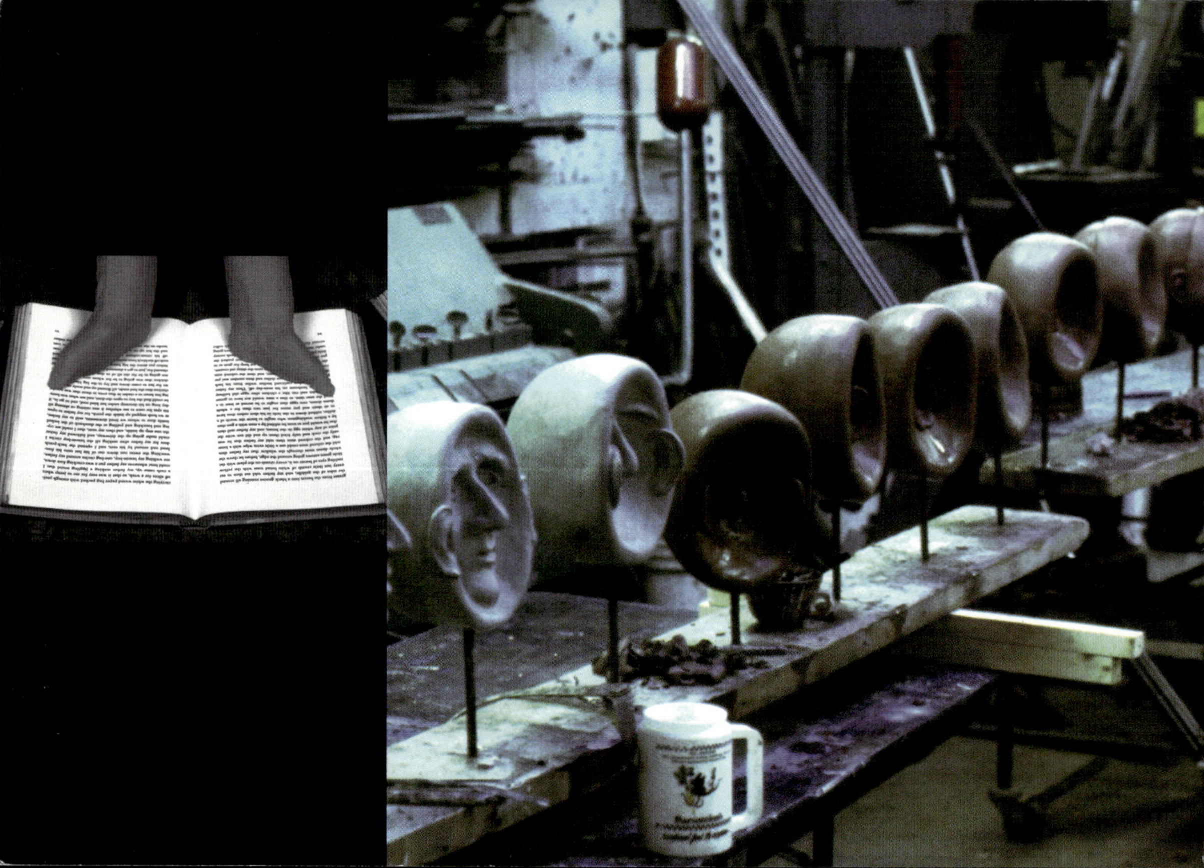

Innuendo Non Troppo: The Work of Gregory Barsamian

Organized by the Contemporary Arts Center, Cincinnati, with generous support from Star Bank. Support for this exhibition catalogue provided by a grant from the Elizabeth Firestone-Graham Foundation.

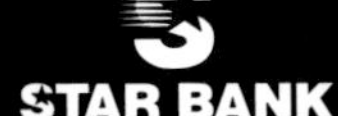

STAR BANK

Curator: David J. Brown

As one of the first contemporary art museums in the United States, Cincinnati's Contemporary Arts Center has long been a progressive cultural force for both its tri-state region and the nation. Founded in 1939, the Center continues to surprise, challenge, educate, and entertain audiences by presenting and exploring the art of today.

The Contemporary Arts Center gratefully acknowledges the continuing support of its members, the Fine Arts Fund, and the City of Cincinnati. A portion of the Center's operating funds is provided through a grant from the Institute of Museum and Library Services, a Federal agency serving the public by strengthening museums and libraries. The Center also receives partial funding from the Ohio Arts Council, a state agency created to foster and encourage the development of the arts and to preserve Ohio's cultural heritage. Funding from the Ohio Arts Council is an investment of state tax dollars that promotes economic growth, educational excellence and cultural enrichment for all Ohioans.

▲ Delta Air Lines   Delta Airlines, the official airline of the Contemporary Arts Center.

Copyright ©1998 The Contemporary Arts Center
Illustrations copyright ©1998
Published by the Contempory Arts Center.
115 East Fifth Street, Cincinnati, Ohio 45202
513.345.8400   http://www.spiral.org

Design: Robin Perl, Perlgraphic, 718.384.2979, perlr@earthlink.net
Printing: Prints Charming Printers, Waldoboro, Maine
Photography: Gregory Barsamian and Mary Ziegler
Cover Illustration: Robin Perl
Front Cover Image: The Scream (detail) 1998
Back Cover Image: No, Never Alone (detail) 1997

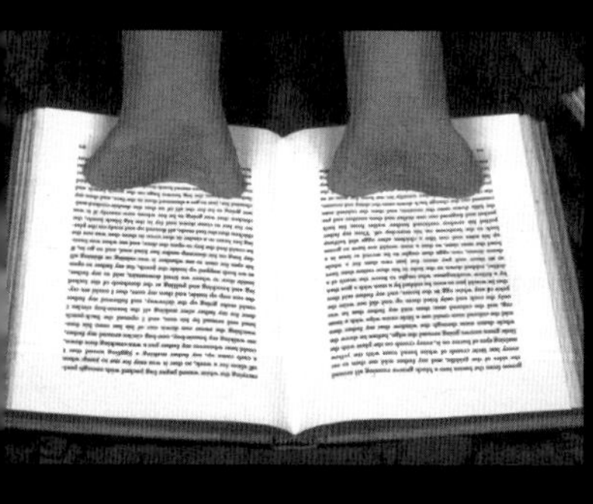

Brown, David J. (David Joseph), 1952-
    Innuendo non troppo: the work of Gregory Barsamian / David J. Brown.–1st ed.
        p. cm.
    Catalog of an exhibition held at the Contemporary Arts Center, Cincinnati, Ohio and five other institutions between Sept. 5, 1998 and May 30, 2000.
    Includes bibliographical references.
    ISBN 0-917562-71-2 (pbk.)
    1. Barsamian, Gregory–Exhibitions. 2. Kinetic sculpture–United States–Exhibitions. I. Barsamian, Gregory. II. Contemporary Arts Center (Cincinnati, Ohio) III. Title.
NB237.B36A4 1998
730' .92–dc21   98-34639
                                                      CIP